GOD'S HAND

IN THE LIFE OF A DREAMER

GOD'S HAND
IN THE LIFE OF A DREAMER

Jimmy Yamada, Jr.

WHITE
MOUNTAIN
CASTLE
PUBLISHING, LLC

www.whitemountaincastle.com
Kapolei, Hawai'i

GOD'S HAND

IN THE LIFE OF A DREAMER

WHITE
MOUNTAIN
CASTLE
PUBLISHING, LLC

White Mountain Castle Publishing, LLC
P.O. Box 700833
Kapolei, Hawaii 96709

Email: whitemountaincastle@yahoo.com
Website: whitemountaincastle.com

Edited by Dawn O'Brien
Cover Design & Text Formatting by Sherrie Dodo-Aguilar
Cover Photos by ©iStockphoto.com
Back Cover Photo by Marc Schecther

ISBN 978-0-9815219-5-4

Printed in Korea

DEDICATION

To Diana who was my rock
when my dreams were my own crazy dreams;
who stood by me when my dreams seemed
to fade in the morning sun;
who believed in me when my dreams came from God.
This took a lot of faith.
She could have chosen a more comfortable life,
but she journeyed with me.
Final destination: heaven on earth.

TABLE OF CONTENTS

PREFACE
viii

CHAPTER 1
GOD SPEAKS TO US IN DREAMS
1

CHAPTER 2
BIBLICAL DREAMS
15

PHOTO GALLERY
41

CHAPTER 3
GOD'S DREAM TOOLKIT
57

CHAPTER 4
A FEW OF MY FAVORITE DREAMS
63

CHAPTER 5
FAMILY DREAMS
83

CHAPTER 6
FRIENDS' DREAMS
103

CHAPTER 7
GOD IS SURE; ARE YOU?
119

PREFACE

BORN TO DREAM

I always had big dreams. Maybe because I was small. My Japanese DNA.

Size doesn't matter in dreamland. My dreams always had to do with whatever was going on around me. If I saw two guys playing and tossing a football, my dream was that I was the star. Another great dreamer moment happened at the zoo: I was throwing peanuts to a bear and caught two grandmas pointing to me and laughing. My imagination took off: Major league baseball pitcher! The crowds will go wild! It lasted a few moments, as most daydreams did, then I was on to the next fantastical episode.

Life had so much going on that I couldn't just pursue one dream. And then came the first dream that was worth really pursuing: Diana. I fell in love with her early, and my dream was to be with her forever. An atheist at that time, forever meant 60 years. Now that we have life in Jesus, forever means forever. **So far it's been over 50 years, and it feels like forever!**

Next dream was building the biggest electrical contracting firm in Hawaii; to work on the biggest buildings. This dream came true as I stood with Diana watching the completion of the Hyatt Regency Waikiki. Both of our sons had their wedding receptions there, and it was like God was bringing me full circle: **Not the biggest buildings, but the strongest family.**

As I look back, I realize God's Hand was moving me and giving me goals, bringing hope and developing my determination. God worked for my good from the very beginning. And, in fact, all of my life. He used my Mom and Dad to nurture my dreams. Yet the initial spark came from my imagination that flamed into full-sized dreams God allowed, nurtured and developed. God was there all along.

PURPOSE OF BOOK

This book is about how God uses dreams and imagination to move us into His Plan.

> *"...His sheep follow Him because they know His voice."*
> (John 10:4)

Jesus is talking to us: we should hear His voice. We should be able to know His voice just as clearly as sheep know the voice of their shepherd. There are many ways God's voice becomes real to us, yet each of us hears Him differently. Dreams are one way. You may also hear God in His Word, the Bible, or through a sermon. My friend Tom Bauer says, "Whatever way you hear Him, just hear Him."

God wants a relationship with us through His Son, Jesus Christ, empowered by the Holy Spirit. A relationship with God — Creator of all — is vibrant, powerful, and life-changing; it goes on 24/7. This relationship would be drudgery if we didn't know and hear His voice clearly.

We see His Hand moving in our lives through all that goes on around us and in us... *if* we are looking. We see this as we rise in the morning and take our first, conscious breath of air, then look out the window to see His glorious creation, and stop a moment to watch the trees growing. We see His Hand moving on our way to work, driving in traffic or riding the bus, or walking up stairs. We enjoy His goodness as we work, as we play, as we raise our families, minister, and fellowship. This is standard fare, 24/7. And as we witness His hand in it all, we thank Him continuously.

This is not a matter of attitude, but a realization: **That the One who spoke the entire Universe into existence wants a relationship with us.** That He would bother to look in our direction? That He would even smile once at us? That He would notice us? That should blow our minds! But too often it does not. Why? We are wretched and take God for granted.

TAKING GOD FOR GRANTED

When I first saw Diana, it was like a Big Bang, when Jesus spoke: *"Hayabunga!* Let the universe be created!"* I imagine Jesus with arms lifted upwards and outward, the whole universe flashing together, lighting up the universe. (I'm sure the moment was even more spectacular than I can imagine.)

Something similar struck my soul as it hit me: *"Diana Enokawa is here!"* We dated and she rocked my world. She was always on my daydreaming mind. When I got home, I could hardly wait to call her. That was late 1962, when phones were plugged into the wall and we had a "party line," which means the houses next door were on the same line. No cell phones. No internet.

Fast forward to 1973, we were married and she still rocked my world; but I was a Vice President of A-1 A-Lectrician and important (in my mind). Something happens to our souls when we think we are important. I was a fool; I didn't believe God existed. In the corporate world, I had gained responsibility, authority, and even a measure of notoriety. I was great in my own eyes. No one else noticed.

At the same time, I started taking Diana for granted. It happened very subtly: I was busy with the business and the kids started coming and becoming central to our lives. Diana's importance seemed to slip. It's not that I didn't love her, but the way I treated her was not pleasing to God. Of course, I didn't realize it then. I was a fool.

As I reflect on this, I realize how easy it is to take God for granted, too. As we live our lives —marry, have kids, start businesses or rise up the workplace ladder, and get involved in ministry — God starts to slip in importance. Jesus puts it this way: **"You don't love Me or each other as you did at first!"** (Rev. 2:4 NLT).

But God doesn't give up on us. He is always with us, even prior to salvation. There is never a second of our existence that God isn't thinking about us with love, favor, grace, mercy, goodness, kindness, and patience as He waits for our response to Him. Each time we get into trouble and cry out to Him, He tingles. Jesus, as He sits next to the Father, may say: "Father, did you hear his cry? Did you hear her?" The Holy Spirit that is with us or living in us (John 14:17) may pray: "God help this wretched sinner, that he may deepen his relationship with You."

Dreams are one way that God draws us to His Son. They also stoke a Holy fire within us, that He may draw us back. God uses dreams to woo us to Himself.

GOD'S PLAN

God has a plan for each of us. He is Sovereign and He alone decides. Yet He still doesn't force us on the path that He knows is best for us. The Bible says, *"He causes all things to work together for our good,"* (Rom. 8:28 NLT). Dreams are one of His great guiding tools: He influences us without our knowing, so we don't feel forced. Ultimately God wants us to know He interacts with us in our world, through things that are important to us. If you want to see God's Hand in your life, just look at what is important in our daily lives: families, businesses, jobs, ministries, friends, even enemies. God is always working in our everyday normal.

DREAMS: KEYS TO GOD'S PLAN

Dreams and visions, our imagination, hopes and desires are important ways God works in our lives. They help us on our mission: *"In his heart a man plans his course, but the Lord determines his steps,"* (Prov. 16:9). Once God sets our hearts on a course (dream), He can readily guide our steps.

Our life course is strategically important and God desires that we end up on the right course. At His disposal are many tools to guide us: God uses our parents, siblings, friends, job, business, the media; everything. (I'm glad I don't have His job!)

The Bible tells us that God's ultimate goal is to be in relationship with us. And He uses dreams to accomplish that. All of the dreams in the Bible were sent by God. **All people have dreams and the Bible has many dreamers:** kings, pharaohs, prophets, His chosen people, enemies of Israel, a cupbearer, a baker, and Joseph. Some dreamers were good and righteous, some were not. Some loved God, some did not. Dreams are universal. The common denominator? **God.** He sends dreams to accomplish what He wants.

In some cases, God wanted the recipient of the dream to do something; in other cases, He wanted the recipient to stop what he was doing, or change course. In many cases, God's dream was given to someone, but another heard or interpreted the dream and took action. God's Hand authors dreams. He is Sovereign and He alone decides how He will use the dream. Dreams can help us recognize that God knows what is going on and He will be with us. Whoever starts his journey being open to hearing from God can easily be guided by Him through dreams.

The goal of this book is for you to live with a full understanding of dreamland. God is causing all things to work together for someone's good; **my aim is to have that someone be *you*!**

I pray you recognize God is working through the dreams He downloads in you — consciously, sub-consciously, even unconsciously. God hopes to deepen your relationship with Him as you interact through dreams. He longs to hear you call for Him to confirm direction, mission, or assignment; that way you may be in His will as you live life for Him. Moreover, I pray you realize that God has been wooing you in dreams and visions all along.

Question: *As God woos you with dreams,* **how does this activate your faith?**

LIFE THROUGH A DREAMER'S EYES

"Although Joseph recognized his brothers,they did
not recognize him.
*Then he **remembered his dreams** about them and said to them,*
'You are spies! You have come to see where our land
is unprotected.'"
(Gen. 42:8-9)

Joseph had *déjà vu* when his brothers came before him. A **flashback** to a dream he had as a child that was actually a **flash forward** to this very moment as adults. God gave Joseph a glimpse of their future.

Almost everyone has had *déjà vu*. This experience which puzzles most people is easily explained by God who is Omniscient. God knows all, the past, present, and future. He knows every event, every thought, every situation that each of us will encounter. He sees everything we will see; He knows how we will feel when we step into the event. I believe He chooses significant situations or events from our future and downloads a snapshot or video of them into our soul. He intends to use these "snapshot" events to get our attention. We may be oblivious to what that is, until now.

Eventually we see a scene, come upon an event, encounter a situation and God activates the "snapshot," *déjà vu* scene in our mind. We feel like we've seen it, been there or done that before.

God is connecting us to Himself through these experiences. He wants us to know He is wooing us, and has always been with us. He's calling us — as if He's jumping up and down, waving His arms and shouting: "I Love you! I'm thinking of you! I planned this from your beginning so that you know I'm in control of all things. I'm proving to you that I know all things and can see your future before it happens. My proof is that you will feel you've seen the scene before. That's Me!"

Jesus said it this way: *"I am telling you now before it happens, so that when it does happen you will believe that I am He"* (John 13:19). Jesus said this to His disciples, as they were about to betray Him. However, Jesus was also speaking directly to us, His **ultimate logic:** When I tell you your future, then it will happen and *"**you will believe that I am He.**"*

God reveals our future through the Bible prophecies, but He also does so personally: *déjà vu.*

Once we understand this mysterious *déjà vu* experience comes from God, we can come to the full and greater realization: **God is with us!** When we connect the dots that all good things go back to God's Hand, **our faith grows!** Our relationship with Him goes beyond begging (we call it "praying," it sounds better). Asking with faith takes on a new life with Christ. We believe He knows all, so when we don't get what we "beg" for, we have the best answer: God saying, "Patience. Right now I'm developing faith in you. I want you to become like my Son." **Miracle provisions are nice, but becoming like Jesus is the ultimate good** (Rom. 8:28-30).

WHAT ARE GOD'S DREAMS?

Those who know God works always for their good can then dream God-sized dreams, not for themselves, but in accordance with God's will. They can dream that one day their whole family will come to know Jesus. They can dream of the transformation of a whole community. We can dream that our churches will become powerhouses of prayer. We can dream that our children will have faith greater than ours and want only what God would want. **We can dream and dream as God dreams.**

Eventually we hear from God and He gives us a clear mission that connects with the big dreams we always had. And God's supernatural power moves in every move we make. We can dream of people being healed emotionally and physically and many coming to the Lord. We can dream of businesspeople having supernatural wisdom to make tons of money, and give most of it away; because they try to "out-give" God but find that they are losing. (And in losing, they win!) We can dream that ordinary Christians living with extraordinary love and wisdom will transform their marketplace.

We can dream of people with supernatural wisdom being elected or appointed to government, and God helping them with policies, laws, and even applying the Constitution properly. People have been dreaming that God heals our land. They never thought God would use them to heal the land. We can dream that God bless America again and not frustrate our leaders. We can dream that people of all races, cultures, languages, religions would be able to work together for our children's sake. We can dream that this would result in the mightiest revival in all history, just before the return of Jesus Christ.

Best of all we can dream that this will not just be a dream.

1

GOD SPEAKS TO US IN DREAMS

"For God does speak
— now one way, now another —
though man may not perceive it.
*In a **dream**, in a **vision of the night**,*
*when **deep sleep** falls on men as they **slumber** in their beds…."*
(Job 33:14-15)

GOD SPEAKS WHEN WE'RE FAST ASLEEP?

For wives whose husbands don't have time for a daily dose of conversation; especially wives who feel their husbands fail to listen: Wait until they fall asleep, then tell them *everything!* This is the one time when your husband won't argue, offer opinions, or snicker as you pour out your heart.

I'm being silly, of course, no husband can listen while he sleeps. Or can they?

*"Why do you complain to him that he answers none of man's words? For God does speak — now one way, now another — though man may not perceive it. In a **dream**, in a **vision** of the night, when **deep sleep** falls on*

men as they **slumber** in their beds, he may speak in their ears and terrify them with warnings, to turn man from wrongdoing and keep him from pride, to preserve his soul from the pit, his life from perishing by the sword. Or a man may be chastened on a bed of pain with constant distress in his bones." (Job 33:13-19)

Unfortunately wives, unless you are God, this doesn't work. A better idea? Pray and let God speak to your husband in dreams. Your husband will know God visited him at night and that may "wake him up."

God speaks to us through His Word about 90% of the time (I'm a numbers guy); but He also speaks in many other ways. According to God, He speaks to us even though we are in "**deep sleep**" through "**dreams**" or "**visions**." In general, a Biblical **dream** takes place when we are asleep. A Biblical **vision** takes place when we are awake and aware.

GOD GIVES *ALL* PEOPLE DREAMS

Indeed the Bible teaches that God communicates through dreams; however, that does not make the people who receive dreams any more special than those who do not. As we see in Joel 2:28 and Acts 2:17, God went from a **faucet flow** of dreams to a **Niagara Falls gush**. Jesus opened the floodgates enabling **all** to be saved and be like Him. **God, through the Holy Spirit, gives dreams to *all* people**. The real bonanza is that God's infinite power is available to all as we live for Him: signs and wonders; wisdom, knowledge, faith, gifts of healing, miraculous powers, prophecy, distinguishing between spirits, speaking and interpretation of tongues (1 Cor. 12:7-11). Dreams are just one part of God working good for us, but an important part, as we shall see.

First, a significant clue about dreams:

> "At once the Lord said to Moses, Aaron and Miriam, 'Come out to the Tent of Meeting, all three of you.' So the three of

them came out. Then the Lord came down in a pillar of cloud; he stood at the entrance to the Tent and summoned Aaron and Miriam. When both of them stepped forward, he said, 'Listen to my words: When a prophet of the Lord is among you, I **reveal myself to him in visions, I speak to him in dreams***.*

"But this is not true of my servant Moses; he is faithful in all my house. **With him I speak face to face, clearly and not in riddles;** *he sees the form of the Lord. Why then were you not afraid to speak against my servant Moses?'*

"The anger of the Lord burned against them, and he left them." (Num. 12:4-9)

One key clue from this passage: **When God speaks in dreams, they're like riddles**. Dreams aren't always easy to understand. **The context of our lives provides the foundation for our dreams.** Yet everyone has so many things going on that a reference point isn't always clear. Is God addressing my family, ministry, job, spouse, children, or others? Is He trying to shape my character? Is He teaching me something? It would be simpler if He just sent an email, but God is not always concerned with simple.

A basic hermeneutics lesson: **Let the Bible interpret the Bible**. This also applies to dreams. We glimpse what dreams may mean by looking at the Bible — God can be counted on to have similar meaning in the use of word pictures (metaphors) in Scripture. For example: yeast, bread, birds, fig trees, and seas, just to name a few. Recognizing His metaphors helps us understand our own dreams.

OPENING THE WATER HYDRANTS

"'In the last days,' God says, **'I will pour out my Spirit on all people. Your sons and daughters will prophesy, your young men will see visions, your old men will dream dreams.** *Even on my servants, both men and women, I will*

pour out my Spirit in those days, and they will prophesy.'"
(Acts 2:17-18)

In the Old Testament, God spoke in special ways to a select few and
His chosen prophets. In the Last Days, God is pouring out His Holy
Spirit on **all people. Everyone!**

And it's not limited to just Christians or Jews:

"For John baptized with water, but in a few days you will be
baptized with the Holy Spirit." (Acts 1:5)
"But you will receive power when the Holy Spirit comes on
you." (Acts 1:8)
"All of them were filled with the Holy Spirit." (Acts 2:4)

These verses lead to the first verse in this section, Acts 2:17-18. **Everyone in the world has dreams.** This is the result of the outpouring
of the Holy Spirit. **God is sending these dreams.**

UNDERSTANDING DREAMS REQUIRES FAITH

We know we have salvation through faith in Christ, but that's just
the beginning of new life. The Bible encourages us to grow far beyond
that in faith:

*"Stand firm in your **faith**."* (Isa. 7:9)
*"The righteous live by **faith**."* (Hab. 2:4)
Jesus on worry: *"O you of little **faith**?"* (Mt. 6:30)
Jesus: *"I have not found anyone in Israel with such great*
***faith**."* (Mt. 8:10)
Jesus: *"According to your **faith** will it be done to you."* (Mt. 9:29)
Jesus: *"When the Son of Man comes, will he find **faith** on*
the earth?" (Luke 18:8)

Dreams are a means of God communicating with us. He wants us
to know something, correct something, direct us to do something,

change course, slow down, turn left, stop and more. **Faith is required in recognizing and understanding dreams from God.** A person with faith believes God when He said He would send dreams. A person of faith is hungry to hear from God and wants to obey God, so he wants to know what dreams mean.

"Jesus told him, 'Because you have seen me, you have believed; blessed are those who have not seen and yet have believed'" (Jn. 20:29). In getting through tough parts of life, I often ask people: "Is Jesus enough? Or do you need continual proof?" Do we need Jesus *plus* our prayers answered? Jesus *plus* a successful business? Jesus *plus* good kids? Jesus *plus* blessings? **Is Jesus enough?** Do we need Jesus to hold our hand and show up in person, or is His presence enough? Dreams help to confirm His presence and grow our faith, if we believe that He speaks in dreams.

Husbands: When you come home and your wife is slamming doors in the house and other things too, do you try to understand her? Or just leave? Do you make yourself useful and look for an opening? Is it the kids? The bills? Did something happen? Do you ask yourself: *"Is it something I did, or more likely did not do?"* If you retreat to your room and just go to sleep, you won't understand what she's trying to tell you. Same with God: **We need to take the extra step of faith** to understand what He is saying.

4 PRACTICAL WAYS TO HEAR GOD IN DREAMS:

1. PRAYER: "SPEAK, LORD!"

First and foremost, ask God to speak to you in dreams. When you ask in faith, expect God to answer. It makes a big difference, **expecting God to answer.** And if you don't ask for something specific, how will you know if He answered? I always ask God for parking spots. If I find one right in front, I know God answered. If I don't ask Him, I might think I was lucky and not credit prayer. If I don't get parking, God speaks loudly: "Wait; you need to develop patience! Walk; you need exercise." God *always* answers.

God wants us to ask Him for all things. James says we don't have because we don't ask God. He also connects our ask to our motives: It can't be for our pleasure (Jas. 4:2-3). When I first became a Christian, I used to ask for financial and material blessings, as well as other blessings for myself. I realize now I don't have to ask God for those things: **He always provides!** Now I ask for things that affect my family, ministry, work and others. Dreams are one way I ask for God's guidance.

2. OBEDIENCE

My wife, Diana, and I have been together since 1962 and we know each other well. She even knows what I will do and will not do. If she thought I would not follow-up on something she wanted me to do, she would not ask; she just did it herself. God is like that. If He thinks you will not obey, He might not give you a dream. He might not communicate if your ears are closed and not paying attention.

For many years, I was a control freak. (I'm getting better, my kids say, "Dad is now at a level five, on a scale of 1-10." Of course, I realize that even if I had improved 50%, a monster is a monster.) At times, Diana hesitated, still not allowed to react in total freedom. She sensed my old pride (a diehard!), especially as I tried to be right in handling ministry and people. The truth is I'm wrong when I think God cannot work through Diana. God once asked me, "**Do you want to be right or righteous?**" I realized that I wanted Diana to be free to hear from God and move as He wills.

Since then, I've worked harder on allowing Diana more freedom in expressing her ideas. It also means she's more free to ask me to do simple things, things she may not have expected me to do 10 years ago. And I believe this blesses God, and our ministry is also blessed.

We must trust God and have an *"all in"* **attitude**; then He's free to send more.

ASK ME & I WILL

"From everyone who has been given much, much will be demanded; and from the one who has been entrusted with much, much more will be asked." (Luke 12:48)

Early in our Christian walk, God blessed us and asked for something in return: a tithe. Truth be told, it belongs to Him and we're giving back what is His. And as He "entrusts" things of greater worth and value to us — families, businesses, wealth, wisdom, Spiritual gifts — He desires our attitude be: **"Ask Lord, and I will do it!"**

As we approach this stage in our Christian journey, God can do great things through us.

Now, please know, I'm not even close to this. For example, there are many places that are not on my "Bucket List": Africa, Mongolia, Russia, and Iraq. Likewise many aspects of ministry are not on my "Bucket List" (I'm too shame to even name them). My mindset limits what God can do through me. Too often, I need to know what He wants first; then I let Him slooowly drag me forward. I miss Kingdom opportunities because I am not 100% *"all in."* Thank God for grace. However, we all strive to be "all in" for the All in All. And someday, we may say, "Ask Lord; **DONE!**"

3. DREAM CLARITY REQUIRES A COMPLETE PICTURE

To understand what God is communicating, we need a complete picture, which is where journaling comes into play. If I don't write them down, these dreams fade fast, like all things dependent on memory. Dreams are fresh when I awake, but as I start my morning routine, the probability of remembering them decreases exponentially. In mere minutes, they've evaporated with the morning mist.

God often communicates over a series of dreams and time. If I see a repeating pattern, it becomes clear that God is telling me something. Could be big or could be small. The big thing is not the dream but knowing that the Almighty God wants to communicate with puny me. Once I realize what He might be saying, I try to make the connection to my concept of "living life." Where does this dream fit: My family? Business? Church ministry, family or programs? My journey with Him? These provide the context.

I find that I do prayer, meditation, worship best during morning exercises. Gravity has been pulling on my body for 67 years and it's winning. My body is sagging, my skin is drooping, my chin has marks and lumps; all from gravity. Now I spend close to 45 minutes with the Lord fighting the earth's force. It also gives me time to hear Him, especially on dreams. How can that be bad?

And, worship music is on as soon as I get up to help me focus on God. I used to listen to messages during this time, but now I find worshipping is more effective. I strive to discern what He wants — in my mission, my daily assignment, my family, Cedar AOG programs, my upcoming message, etc. I have no formula. God sometimes shows up and brings clarity. Essentially, it takes effort and discipline.

4. DREAMS PROVIDE CONFIRMATION

Our life's mission has many paths and assignments: family, job, business, ministry, etc. As God looks at our lives, He can guide our steps in many ways, including dreams. When we hit a roadblock or need guidance, we may ask Him and He will answer. If we're off track, He will correct.

GIDEON'S CONFIRMATION

One effective way is to lay a fleece before God. Israel cried out to God when they were oppressed by the Midianites. God gave Gideon the call to save the Israelites, but Gideon had to be sure it was God:

"Gideon replied, 'If now I have found favor in your eyes, give me a sign that it is really you talking to me.'" (Judg. 6:17)

"Gideon said to God, 'If you will save Israel by my hand as you have promised — look, I will place a wool fleece on the threshing floor. If there is dew only on the fleece and all the ground is dry, then I will know that you will save Israel by my hand, as you said.' And that is what happened. Gideon rose early the next day; he squeezed the fleece and wrung out the dew — a bowlful of water.

"Then Gideon said to God, 'Do not be angry with me. Let me make just one more request. Allow me one more test with the fleece. This time make the fleece dry and the ground covered with dew.' That night God did so. Only the fleece was dry; all the ground was covered with dew." (Judg. 6:36-40)

There's much ado regarding Gideon's "lack of courage." Because he asked God for a sign, people think it shows a lack of faith or a sign of fear. Gideon actually had great faith. He just needed confirmation that **it really was the Lord calling him**. The laying of the fleece was confirmation that it was the Lord *beyond any shadow of a doubt*. Once he had that confirmation, he went *"all in."* He obeyed the Lord and cut down the Asherah pole and his father's altar to Baal. Sure, he was still afraid, so he did it at night. However, that's courage, moving ahead despite fear. That's obedience, doing what God commands.

The Midianites had so many men it was *"impossible to count"* (Judg. 6:5). Gideon had only 32,000 men but further obeyed God's command and released all but 300 trusty soldiers. **Whoa!** Imagine the faith that took! Gideon was far from a wimpy commander; he had **powerful faith** in a mighty God.

In my own life, there have been times when God was leading my course yet also redirecting my steps. I knew both my ultimate mission and present journey, yet He changed my specific path. So I laid out a fleece: I asked God to either confirm in a dream. One such dream included our son Daven.

SURFING THE NATIONS

Daven was leading a Bible study in our home and invited his friends for fun games, food, fellowship, worship and God. Unbeatable combination. Plus Diana took care of the food. Unbeatable cook!

The study started with a handful and grew to a dozen. That's when God connected us to **Tom and Cindy Bauer** and the Christian organization, **Surfing the Nations**. Now, anything Tom and Cindy are involved in automatically becomes fertile ground for youth. By early 2003, the Bible study was averaging 25-40 young adults.

God started planting the idea for me to get more involved in Men's Ministry. He used His usual communication by sending a mental text: "Think about men." In late June 2003, there was a men's movement all around, especially at First Assembly of God. On Saturday July 19, **Pastor Klayton Ko** hosted a men's barbecue. (B.Y.O.S! Bring Your Own Steak! I brought a vegan steak. So manly!) That served as a prelude to Sunday, when Pastor Ko preached a stronger connection with men.

That night, God was tugging on my heart. But since I was busy (who isn't?!) I didn't want to do more without adjusting my schedule. God had already been preparing us for the next step: A few months before, we had almost 80 youth on our back lanai and adjoining walkway. And 70% were packed like sardines on the lanai. Amazing! Yet I thought (another God text), *I wonder if the lanai could collapse?* A look at the support structures confirmed it was fine. That night was an anomaly; we'd never come close to that number! God was nudging me.

That night, I asked God to give me a dream. If He wanted me to redirect and stop the Bible study so I could be more involved with men, "Then give me a dream." Here's what happened next from my previous book, "God's Hand in the Life of an Electrician":

"That night I had a dream involving Pastor Ko and Pastor Ernie. In the dream, we were at our A-1A warehouse and Pastor Ko climbed up one of the posts holding up the warehouse, then held on tightly at the top. The dream shifted to Pastor Ernie and me. We were holding one end of a ten-foot length of four-inch rigid conduit (metal pipe used for electrical wiring), weighing approximately 50 pounds. We were running as if we were racing another team, though there was no one else. After ten feet, we suddenly dropped the conduit. The dream ended and I awoke.

"I realized God had given me direction and the interpretation was clear: **We were letting men in the church fall through our grasp**."

I now had the unpleasant task of notifying the Bauers. What I didn't know was that the pastor of Grace Bible wanted to move the study to their Kalihi property, where Surfing the Nations was located. But Tom told Cindy, "Jimmy will be hurt."

Tom was away in Bali that month so I called Cindy that next Tuesday, July 22. Before I could say a word, Cindy said she was glad I called because God had impressed on her to move the study to Kalihi. She did something she never does: took action without Tom. It would have been a sad day had I not asked God for confirmation. We all would have "played nice," to avoid hurting each others' feelings (except God's). And I wouldn't have added a men's meeting.

Has this ever happened to you?

Many people serve God with all their heart but not in His perfect will, all because they keep doing what God first called them to do. They cannot hear His course changes and redirect. Many still serve, however, not in the area God wants. **Christianity is a**

living relationship with God, one in which we are in constant communication with Him and in which we get to hear from Him often. Especially at critical turning points! It doesn't have to be through dreams, but hear His voice. Tom would say, "Whatever way you get it, just get it!"

PRACTICAL FOUNDATION FOR DREAMS

Clearly God uses dreams; but, the Million-Dollar Question is: *Are all dreams from God?* The Bible does not answer this so allow me to present my opinion. (I love this! No one can definitively rebut.☺)

Let's quickly recap to give context for the Million-Dollar Answer: **The main purpose of dreams is God revealing Himself to us so we may take action.** He also reveals our future to help us with mission and direction. And God confirms current direction or shows us course correction.

Now, a number of issues come up with dreams:

First: Men confess that they have dreams about drugs/alcohol, or sex with women who are not their wives. My answer? **God is revealing what you are thinking about**; what's on your mind. God is not tempting you nor prophesying, He doesn't do that. He is revealing your inner thoughts and character. Change! Repent and take captive every thought so that you may fix your mind on the things above.

Second: All people have dreams that don't seem to have any special meaning, and even seem foolish and senseless. My opinion: **God is just talking story**. It's like hanging out with a friend: If you only have deep discussions and no joy, joking or laughter, you're missing out. Jesus had fun and a sense of humor. When God sends silly dreams, He's having fun. Another possibility? We simply don't understand the dream. That doesn't mean God is not communicating through the dream. Listen closely.

Third: **God uses dreams to reveal our fears**. One recurring dream I had when I was young: I was at the Old Stadium (aka "Termite Palace") in Honolulu. I'm seated near the top and from the opposite end a giant Tyrannosaurus Rex dinosaur busts in and comes straight for me. In terror, I clamber to the top of the stadium, jump over, and begin falling, falling, falling...suddenly I wake up.

To this day, I hate the sense of falling. In fact, when we go to Disneyland and jump on the "Pirates of the Caribbean" ride, I know when the "big dip" is coming, grab the rails, squeeze my eyes shut and panic. In reality, it's actually a pretty small dip: It's a child's joy ride! But it triggers my nightmare. God reveals my fear of being out of control, and assures me He is in control. On Christ the solid rock I stand! What do your bad dreams reveal about you? What is God trying to shine the light upon in your life?

Fourth: Through dreams, **God reveals our stand for righteousness**. I've had dreams where I'm in a bar or at a party and I'm not drinking. God showed me He knows where I am as far as these substances and way of life. I've been delivered from heavy-duty drinking and partying. Thank God!

Fifth: **God sends warning dreams to caution us**. Diana remembers a dream when she was young and at the Kress Store in Fort Street Mall. (It was torn down in the 60s.) She was going to "borrow" some trinkets and she saw a bright light appear. She never stole anything even though her friends did.

You may have more types of dreams with different issues. All dreams are from God. Lean in and hear what He is saying. Take God's revelations in your dreams seriously. You'll be amazed!

This first chapter on dreams sets a sure, strong foundation: Dreams reveal God is in living, constant communication with us. Possibly the most mysterious of God's voice choices is through dreams. So we also covered challenges within dreams. Yet this is not a book about dreams, **it's about God: God drawing us closer to Himself**. Next, we'll look at dreams recorded in the Bible as they provide symbols and metaphors for our own dreams.

2

BIBLICAL DREAMS

"I make known the end from the beginning,
from ancient times, what is still to come.
I say: My purpose will stand,
and I will do all that I please.
From the east I summon a bird of prey;
*from a far-off land, **a man to fulfill my purpose.***
What I have said, that will I bring about;
what I have planned, that will I do.
Listen to me, you stubborn-hearted,
you who are far from righteousness.
I am bringing my righteousness near, it is not far away;
and my salvation will not be delayed.
I will grant salvation to Zion,
my splendor to Israel."
(Isaiah 46:10-13)

The Bible reveals a God who uses dreams sent at the perfect time to the perfect person and culminating in the perfect result. The people that He sent dreams to cross lines: some were kings, others were servants or slaves. Some recognized God, some did not. Some were Jewish, others were not. Some had good intentions, some did not. God is sovereign and may use anyone as He pleases.

In this chapter, we'll examine 11 Biblical dreams, using simple summaries to highlight God's truth. We'll seek lessons that may apply to our own lives. In Isaiah, God promises to use *"a man to fulfill my purpose."* He does that to this very day and He wants to use you, if you'll allow Him.

Here are the 11 dreams and the men and women God used:

1. GOD PROTECTS ABRAHAM

After the destruction of Sodom and Gomorrah, Abraham moved to Gerar, where Abimelech, king of Gerar, lived. Abraham said Sarah (his wife) was his sister so the king took her because of her beauty. *"But God came to Abimelech in a **dream** one night and said to him, 'You are as good as dead because of the woman you have taken; she is a married woman'"* (Gen. 20:3). *Abimelech was innocent, and he told the Lord so: "Then God said to him in the dream, 'Yes, I know you did this with a clear conscience, and so I have kept you from sinning against me. That is why I did not let you touch her. Now return the man's wife, for he is a prophet, and he will pray for you and you will live. But if you do not return her, you may be sure that you and all yours will die'"* (Gen. 20:6-7).

Abimelich acted immediately: He called Abraham into his court, ripped into him, returned Sarah and sent them off with sheep, cattle, and slaves. Plus a thousand shekels of silver. *"Then Abraham prayed to God, and God healed Abimelech"* (Gen. 20:17).

Abimelech was not part of the Hebrew nation, yet God spoke to him in a dream to protect and bless Abraham. Notice that Abraham wasn't involved in the dream or its interpretation. Dreams are not only for "holy people." God is sovereign and may use anyone He pleases. He always fulfills His purpose.

The second great Biblical dream comes soon after with Abraham's son, Jacob.

2. STAIRWAY TO HEAVEN

When Jacob's mother, Rebekah, learned that Esau wanted to kill Jacob, she sent him away. Jacob left for Haran to stay with family. He stopped to sleep and God gave a dream as a prophecy to sustain him:

> "He had a dream in which he saw a stairway resting on the earth, with its top reaching to heaven, and the angels of God were ascending and descending on it. There above it stood the Lord, and he said: 'I am the Lord, the God of your father Abraham and the God of Isaac. I will give you and your descendants the land on which you are lying. Your descendants will be like the dust of the earth, and you will spread out to the west and to the east, to the north and to the south. All peoples on earth will be blessed through you and your offspring. **I am with you** and will watch over you wherever you go, and I will bring you back to this land. I will not leave you until I have done what I have promised you.'
>
> "When Jacob awoke from his sleep, he thought, 'Surely the Lord is in this place, and I was not aware of it.' He was afraid and said, 'How awesome is this place! This is none other than the house of God; this is the gate of heaven.'" (Gen. 28:12-17)

As Jacob ran for his life, the Lord revealed Himself in a personal way and said, "**I am with you.**" How great is that! This touched Jacob immensely as he realized that the Lord was always there, even if "*I was not aware of it.*" And to top it off, God showed Jacob that he would be a connection between earth and heaven; a prophecy that pointed beyond Jacob's current situation all the way to Christ!

The Lord may be speaking the same to you: "I am with you. I live in you." And like Jacob in his desperation, our hearts burst as we realize, *I was not aware of it. How **awesome** is this place!*

3. GOD COMES TO LABAN IN A DREAM

Jacob arrived finally at his Uncle Laban's land. Because Uncle Laban was a switch-and-bait swindler, Jacob was tricked into marrying Laban's firstborn daughter Leah. And then Uncle Laban negotiated another seven years of conscripted labor for Jacob's true love, Laban's second daughter, Rachel. Despite even more family drama, Jacob worked faithfully and his family and his flocks increased. (There's great reward for working as the Bible directs us, as *"unto the Lord,"* even for corrupt employers!)

Eventually God gave Jacob permission to return to the land of his fathers. So Jacob took his family and flock and snuck off without telling his uncle. Laban pursued Jacob with an army (all relatives) and as they caught up: *"God came to Laban the Aramean in a **dream** at night and said to him, 'Be careful not to say anything to Jacob, either good or bad'"* (Gen. 31:24). God stopped Laban in his tracks.

Laban lamented and then lambasted Jacob: *"You've carried off my daughters like captives in war..."* (Gen. 31:26). Then Laban blasted and boasted about his ability to harm Jacob, except for one huge catch: *"But last night the God of your father said to me, 'Be careful not to say anything to Jacob, either good or bad'"* (Gen. 31:29). God saved Jacob via a dream. God may also choose to protect you by visiting others in their dreams and disrupting their plans against you.

And as the pages of the Bible turn, God's plan unfurls for Jacob's destiny through more dreams...

4. JOSEPH'S DREAM

Jacob ended up having 11 sons, the youngest was named Joseph. God had given Jacob a new name, Israel. Joseph was Israel's favorite and everyone knew it; unfortunately, so did his older brothers: *"They hated him and could not speak a kind word to him"* (Gen. 37:4).

Joseph had two dreams:

> *"Joseph had a dream, and when he told it to his brothers, they hated him all the more. He said to them, 'Listen to this dream I had: We were binding sheaves of grain out in the field when suddenly my sheaf rose and stood upright, while your sheaves gathered around mine and bowed down to it.' His brothers said to him, 'Do you intend to reign over us? Will you actually rule us?' And they hated him all the more because of his dream and what he had said.*
>
> *"Then he had another dream, and he told it to his brothers. 'Listen,' he said, 'I had another dream, and this time the sun and moon and eleven stars were bowing down to me.' When he told his father as well as his brothers, his father rebuked him and said, 'What is this dream you had? Will your mother and I and your brothers actually come and bow down to the ground before you?' His brothers were jealous of him, but his father kept the matter in mind."* (Gen. 37:5-11)

It's not clear if Joseph understood the dream but what is clear is that his brothers were upset. God had given Joseph's father and brothers the interpretation: Joseph would reign over them all. Only Israel *"kept the matter in mind."* The brothers became jealous and the family's reaction was to put Joseph down. However, God used it for good: God gave Joseph hope while he went through separation, slavery, and prison. What's more, God knew that Joseph would become an interpreter of dreams. God used this dream experience to give Joseph the faith to interpret dreams for others...

5. DREAMS OF A CUPBEARER & BAKER

Joseph's brothers hated him so badly that they sold him to the Midianites who turned around and sold him to Potiphar, a guard captain for Egypt's Pharaoh. Joseph ended up in jail after refusing Potiphar's wife and her sexual advances. Yet God was even working this out for Joseph and all of Israel, though it may not have been apparent at the time.

The Lord was with Joseph in prison and gave him favor with the warden: He was promoted to be in charge. Then Pharaoh threw two of his officials, a cupbearer and a baker, in prison. By God's design these two key officials ended up under Joseph's custody. **God sent them both dreams.** (Spoiler alert: This was God's plan to get Joseph promoted to Second-in-Command to Pharaoh.)

The cupbearer spoke: *"In my dream I saw a vine in front of me, and on the vine were three branches. As soon as it budded, it blossomed, and its clusters ripened into grapes. Pharaoh's cup was in my hand, and I took the grapes, squeezed them into Pharaoh's cup and put the cup in his hand"* (Gen. 40:9-11).

Joseph interpreted: *"'This is what it means,' Joseph said to him. 'The three branches are three days. Within three days Pharaoh will lift up your head and restore you to your position, and you will put Pharaoh's cup in his hand, just as you used to do when you were his cupbearer'"* (Gen. 40:12-13).

The chief baker also asked Joseph to interpret his dream, expecting a similar interpretation: *"'I too had a dream: On my head were three baskets of bread. In the top basket were all kinds of baked goods for Pharaoh, but the birds were eating them out of the basket on my head.' 'This is what it means,' Joseph said. 'The three baskets are three days. Within three days*

Pharaoh will lift off your head and hang you on a tree. And the birds will eat away your flesh.'"

"Now the third day was Pharaoh's birthday, and he gave a feast for all his officials. He lifted up the heads of the chief cupbearer and the chief baker in the presence of his officials: He restored the chief cupbearer to his position, so that he once again put the cup into Pharaoh's hand, but he hanged the chief baker, just as Joseph had said to them in his interpretation." (Gen. 40:16-23)

Clearly these were prophetic dreams sent by God, and God gave Joseph interpretation. The dreams also give key intel on how God works through dreams:

1. **Interpretation is from God**: *"Joseph said to them, 'Do not **interpretations belong to God? Tell me your dreams'"* (Gen. 40:8).

2. **God speaks in symbols**: *Vine, branches, clusters, grapes, Pharaoh's cup, cupbearer's hands.* Joseph's interpretation for the cupbearer lines up logically:

CUPBEARER'S DREAM

1. Vine with three branches	1. Three days
2. Budded, blossomed, clusters ripened into grapes	2. Pharaoh will lift up your head and restore you to your position
3. Pharaoh's cup was in my hand	3. You will put Pharaoh's cup in his hand
4. I took the grapes and squeezed them into Pharaoh's cup	4. "As you used to do" aka back to normal

The Bible doesn't say how Joseph was given interpretation: Whether God downloaded the definition or if Joseph understood God's language. Had he learned God's symbols because he'd spent so much time with God in his trials? It's hard to say. But here's what is clear: ***"Interpretations belong to God."***

The cupbearer's dream included only life-giving symbols: vines ripened into grapes and grapes squeezed into Pharaoh's cup. Joseph knew God's message from His life-giving symbols meant restoration for the cupbearer.

BAKER'S DREAM

1. Three baskets of bread	1. Three days
2. Baked goods on head	2. Pharaoh will lift off your head and hang you on a tree
3. Birds eating the bread	3. Birds will eat away your flesh

Joseph knew birds as scavengers who eat dead carcasses. He probably knew the story of his great-grandfather, Abram. The Lord came to Abram and promised him to be a father of the nations. When asked for a sign of confirmation, God put Abram into a **deep sleep** and told Abram: *"'Bring me a heifer, a goat and a ram, each three years old, along with a dove and a young pigeon.' Abram brought all these to him, cut them in two and arranged the halves opposite each other; the* **birds***, however, he did not cut in half. Then* **birds of prey** *came down on the carcasses, but Abram drove them away"* (Gen. 15:9-11).

God used the same image-language of birds in the baker's dream and He knew Joseph would know the symbol. Also, they ate the bread while the basket was on his head — sacred territory — to steal food is *not* positive. Joseph knew God's dream for the baker would end badly.

God could have given direct interpretation to Joseph, but God wants a deep relationship with us. Imagine it's like a person who knows their spouse after years of being together: the nuances of body language, words, tone of voice, actions (like crashing of doors, screams of joy or of anguish). God seeks a similar intimate communication with us. Joseph was deeply in love with God and although he didn't have a Bible he knew God intimately and therefore he had a "Living Bible" for interpretation. He learned God's communication by watching life: the sun, moon, trees, vines, grapes, and birds.

"Since the creation of the world God's invisible qualities — his eternal power and divine nature — **have been clearly seen, being understood from what has been made** *so that people are without excuse."* (Rom. 1:20)

Joseph may not have needed God's direct revelation for interpretation; he knew how His God worked and thought. They were on the same wavelength. My wife doesn't have to spell everything out for me. (Well, sometimes!) Joseph knew what God was saying. Similarly, Christians get to be the best dream interpreters. Why? Because we're the best at knowing what God is saying to a hungry world! God sends dreams and we help to connect to life for all to understand.

6. PHARAOH'S DREAM: FAMINE COMING

My team is the San Francisco 49ers. There are 16 games in a normal football schedule. Every game is important, but the final one is the big one, especially if it's Super Bowl. This next Biblical dream is the Super Bowl of all Super Bowls, especially for Joseph. God sent this dream as the ultimate and final promotion for Joseph. And, just to show off a little, God sent it to the very top: to Pharaoh! It started off as just another day in the grunge and drudgery of prison and ended up in the grand and powerful palace! The set-up: It had been two full years since Joseph had interpreted the dream for the cupbearer. Thirteen years since his brothers had sold him in one of the first recorded cases of human trafficking. Then, lightning struck, God sent a dream to a non-Jew:

"Pharaoh had a dream: He was standing by the Nile, when out of the river there came up seven cows, sleek and fat, and they grazed among the reeds. After them, seven other cows,

ugly and gaunt, came up out of the Nile and stood beside those on the riverbank. And the cows that were ugly and gaunt ate up the seven sleek, fat cows. Then Pharaoh woke up.

"He fell asleep again and had a second dream: Seven heads of grain, healthy and good, were growing on a single stalk. After them, seven other heads of grain sprouted — thin and scorched by the east wind. The thin heads of grain swallowed up the seven healthy, full heads. Then Pharaoh woke up...." (Gen. 41:1-7)

Two dreams in the **same night**. Bonus: Anytime God repeats it twice, snap to attention! And on the same night? He's adding an exclamation point!

God used the nightmare to deeply distress Pharaoh, enough that it made him look for someone to help him interpret it. Pharaoh sought out his *"magicians and wise men"* for answers, but to no avail. They were not on God's wavelength. In fact, had they interpreted the dream, Pharaoh would not have had to call Joseph. We may never have seen him again! But that's not God's plan or the end of His Book.

Finally, the cupbearer remembered Joseph and told Pharaoh about the young Hebrew who had an unreal ability to interpret dreams. God called up the cupbearer in the "Super Bowl." God never leaves things to chance: *"What I have planned, that will I do"* (Isa. 10:11).

Joseph entered the arena primed for the Big Game. Though it was a day of destiny, he didn't have to do any heavy lifting or big miracles, he didn't even break a sweat or cop an attitude (for being forgotten). God was weaving everything together for good: all his past dreams and long-suffering, working with the guard captain, being in Pharaoh's Egypt, rising to influence the prisoners and faithfully interpreting others' dreams. This day could not have taken place one day, week, or year earlier; God chose that day:

> "Then Joseph said to Pharaoh, 'The dreams of Pharaoh are one and the same. God has revealed to Pharaoh what he is about to do. The seven good cows are seven years, and the seven good heads of grain are seven years; it is one and the same dream. The seven lean, ugly cows that came up afterward are seven years, and so are the seven worthless heads of grain scorched by the east wind: They are seven years of famine.
>
> "It is just as I said to Pharaoh: God has shown Pharaoh what he is about to do. Seven years of great abundance are coming throughout the land of Egypt, but seven years of famine will follow them. Then all the abundance in Egypt will be forgotten, and the famine will ravage the land. The abundance in the land will not be remembered, because the famine that follows it will be so severe. The reason the dream was given to Pharaoh in two forms is that the matter has been firmly decided by God, and God will do it soon." (Gen. 41:25-32)

Again God used symbols that Pharaoh would understand: cows, the Nile, and grain. Joseph had spiritual eyes to see the symbols and know their Godly meaning. When he translated that to Pharaoh, Joseph was promoted to Second-in-Command. And through that development, Joseph reunited with his family and moved them to Egypt. Consequently, God used those dreams to incubate Israel for 400 years. Dreams are part of God's eternal plan: Not only blessing that person but all people for all time.

Next, we advance in God's Kingdom Come to a famous "coward," Gideon.

7. GIDEON'S DREAM: "GET UP, GO DOWN, & BE ENCOURAGED"

When Gideon understood that God was with him, he went *"all in."* He had 300 men with which to save Israel, he had to know beyond a shadow of a doubt the victory would only be God. We pick up the story where we left off earlier in chapter 1:

> *"The Lord said to Gideon, 'With the three hundred men that lapped I will save you and give the Midianites into your hands. Let all the other men go, each to his own place.' So Gideon sent the rest of the Israelites to their tents but kept the three hundred, who took over the provisions and trumpets of the others.*
>
> *"Now the camp of Midian lay below him in the valley. During that night the Lord said to Gideon, 'Get up, go down against the camp, because I am going to give it into your hands. If you are afraid to attack, go down to the camp with your servant Purah and listen to what they are saying. Afterward, you will be encouraged to attack the camp.' So he and Purah his servant went down to the outposts of the camp. The Midianites, the Amalekites and all the other eastern peoples had settled in the valley, thick as locusts. Their camels could no more be counted than the sand on the seashore.*
>
> *"Gideon arrived just as a man was telling a friend his dream. 'I had a dream,' he was saying. 'A round loaf of barley bread came tumbling into the Midianite camp. It struck the tent with such force that the tent overturned and collapsed.'*
>
> *"His friend responded, 'This can be nothing other than the sword of Gideon son of Joash, the Israelite. God has given the Midianites and the whole camp into his hands.' When Gideon heard the dream and its interpretation, he worshiped God. He returned to the camp of Israel and called out, 'Get up! The Lord has given the Midianite camp into your hands.' Dividing*

the three hundred men into three companies, he placed trum-
pets and empty jars in the hands of all of them, with torches
inside." (Judg. 7:7-16)

God used two dreams at the perfect time so Gideon would be encouraged and nail the time of attack. First, God sent Gideon a dream and
said: *"I am going to give it into your hands."* Gideon heard this and was
sure of impending victory.

Second, the Lord said, *"Listen to what they are saying. Afterward,*
you will be encouraged to attack the camp" (Judg. 7:10). They heard the
discussion about a dream and God used Purah to bring interpretation
to Gideon, a double-confirmation, which is why God had Gideon
take Purah. Clearly God sent the Midianite's dream. And as a result,
Gideon courageously obeyed God, in spite of his fear.

God built Gideon's courage. He also established timing and
strategy: three companies, trumpets and empty jars with torches.
You'll never find that in a West Point strategy book! Gideon was so
invigorated that he lead the charge, saying, *"Follow my lead!"* And
they arrived in God's perfect timing: *"Just after they had changed the*
guard" (Judg. 7:19).

The key to victory was God sending two dreams — one to Gideon
and one to a Midianite — and also providing interpretation. Remember: *"Lord, you established peace for us;* **all that we have accomplished**
you have done for us" (Isa. 26:12). If God says it, He completes it,
even if He says it in dreams. And don't be afraid of being afraid:
God will meet you at your fears as He did with Gideon. God forged a
mighty, victorious, history-making general where once there was just
a guy hiding in a hole. True story! And God even provided a "spotter"
or second person to hear the discussion and confirm its meaning. God
can and will do the same for you.

Charge! *Go forth and dream!*

Moving forward in God's unfurling prophecies, comes one of the most notorious world rulers of all time:

7. GOD REVEALS FUTURE KINGDOMS TO NEBUCHADNEZZAR

Everyone is interested in the future and one of the most important books on the End Times is the book of Daniel. In it God communicates largely through dreams. Specifically, God sent Nebuchadnezzar a deeply troubling dream. So the King summoned his magicians, sorcerers, and astrologers to tell him the dream and give him interpretation. Of course, they said it was impossible! And insisted that he needed to tell them the dream first, then they could interpret. The catch? This dream was so important that Nebuchadnezzar didn't want to risk getting scammed again by his "Dream Team." (figure 1, page 41)

Nebuchadnezzar threatened to cut his astrologers to pieces. God orchestrated the ensuing panic so He could introduce Daniel to give interpretation and get his promotion:

> *"Daniel replied, 'No wise man, enchanter, magician or diviner can explain to the king the mystery he has asked about, but there is a* **God** *in heaven who reveals mysteries. He has shown King Nebuchadnezzar what will happen in days to come. Your dream and the visions that passed through your mind as you lay on your bed are these…. You looked, O king, and there before you stood a large statue — an enormous, dazzling statue, awesome in appearance. The head of the statue was made of pure gold, its chest and arms of silver, its belly and thighs of bronze, its legs of iron, its feet partly of iron and partly of baked clay. While you were watching, a rock was cut out, but not by human hands. It struck the statue on its feet of iron and clay and smashed them. Then the iron, the clay, the bronze, the silver*

and the gold were broken to pieces at the same time and became like chaff on a threshing floor in the summer. The wind swept them away without leaving a trace. But the rock that struck the statue became a huge mountain and filled the whole earth.

"'This was the dream, and now we will **interpret** it to the king. You, O king, are the king of kings. The God of heaven has given you dominion and power and might and glory; in your hands he has placed mankind and the beasts of the field and the birds of the air. Wherever they live, he has made you ruler over them all. You are that head of gold.

"'After you, another kingdom will rise, inferior to yours. Next, a third kingdom, one of bronze, will rule over the whole earth. Finally, there will be a fourth kingdom, strong as iron — for iron breaks and smashes everything — and as iron breaks things to pieces, so it will crush and break all the others. Just as you saw that the feet and toes were partly of baked clay and partly of iron, so this will be a divided kingdom; yet it will have some of the strength of iron in it, even as you saw iron mixed with clay. As the toes were partly iron and partly clay, so this kingdom will be partly strong and partly brittle. And just as you saw the iron mixed with baked clay, so the people will be a mixture and will not remain united, any more than iron mixes with clay.

"'In the time of those kings, the God of heaven will set up a kingdom that will never be destroyed, nor will it be left to another people. It will crush all those kingdoms and bring them to an end, but it will itself endure forever. This is the meaning of the vision of the rock cut out of a mountain, but not by human hands — a rock that broke the iron, the bronze, the clay, the silver and the gold to pieces.

"'The great God has shown the king what will take place **in the future**. The dream is true and the interpretation is trustworthy.'" (Dan. 2:27-45)

Allow me to pause here and point directly to you, dear reader: **God is speaking right here and now through this chapter to us!** God revealed "coming kingdoms":

1. the Babylonian kingdom (head of gold)
2. the Medo-Persian kingdom (chest and arms of silver)
3. the Greek kingdom (belly and thighs of bronze)
4. the Roman kingdom (legs of iron)

One key is found in verse 44: God sets up a Kingdom that can never be destroyed, established in Jesus Christ. God used a **dream** to bring one of the most important prophesies concerning the coming Messiah. To a heathen king! God may use anyone, I pray we step out in faith and be used by Him.

Next we'll look at another part of the book of Daniel where a dream and visions are given from God. By the way, confirmation is a key part of God's Word and His Truth: It can be cross-referenced and verified across many different sources. And history testifies to His Truth: God's prophecies always come true! God also gives the same visions or dreams to multiple sources many times…

9. GOD CONFIRMS COMING KINGDOMS TO DANIEL

"In the first year of Belshazzar king of Babylon, Daniel had a dream, and visions passed through his mind as he was lying on his bed. He wrote down the substance of his dream." (Dan. 7:1)

Critics of prophecy complain that anyone can draw anything out of the Bible. They complain that we see hidden meanings and "reach for straws" to line up Biblical passages to match the events of history. Ultimately, they say, "It's all so arbitrary!"

Correction: That's looking at it from the **wrong perspective.** God chooses the prophecies, we do not. He also selects the events in history that He desires to line up. Further, God purposely does not make the understanding clear for those who pick and choose. However, once we look closely at His illustrations, they become over-whelmingly precise, detailed and clear.

*"No, we speak of **God's secret wisdom**, a **wisdom that has been hidden** and that God destined for our glory before time began"* (1 Cor. 2:7). *Jesus also said He would speak in parables, which are not always clear: "[Jesus] replied, 'The **knowledge of the secrets of the kingdom of heaven** has been given to you, but not to them"* (Mt. 13:11). In these passages, both Paul and Jesus spoke about Jesus' message, the gospel of grace and salvation. It is free to all but there is also hidden, secret wisdom that is only selectively available to a few. The same was true of Bible prophets who spoke in God-given pictures that even they didn't understand! (Like John and the book of "Revelations.") Why? Because God knew as He authored the Bible that there would come a time for revelation. **We now have the ability to understand the prophecies with the events of history unfolding before our very eyes!**

Daniel chapter 7 told of a dream God gave Daniel about the same coming kingdoms that God had given to Nebuchadnezzar in chapter 2. God's dream to Nebuchadnezzar was from his point-of-view to make it directly relevant for him, so God used the image of a giant statue with a gold head. That was how Nebuchadnezzar viewed himself. In contrast, Daniel's dream was from God's point-of-view of the coming kingdoms: all beasts.

"Daniel said: 'In my vision at night I looked, and there before me were the four winds of heaven churning up the great sea. Four great beasts, each different from the others, came up out of the sea. The first was like a lion, and it had the wings of an eagle. I watched until its wings were torn off and it was lifted from the ground so that it stood on two feet like a man, and the heart of a man was given to it. And there before me was a second beast, which looked like a bear. It was raised up

*on one of its sides, and it had three ribs in its mouth between
its teeth. It was told, 'Get up and eat your fill of flesh!'*

*"After that, I looked, and there before me was anoth-
er beast, one that looked like a leopard. And on its
back it had four wings like those of a bird. This beast
had four heads, and it was given authority to rule.*

*"After that, in my vision at night I looked, and there before
me was a fourth beast — terrifying and frightening and very
powerful. It had large iron teeth; it crushed and devoured its
victims and trampled underfoot whatever was left. It was
different from all the former beasts, and it had ten horns.*

*"While I was thinking about the horns, there before me was
another horn, a little one, which came up among them; and
three of the first horns were uprooted before it. This horn had
eyes like the eyes of a man and a mouth that spoke boastfully."*
(Dan. 7:2-8)

Each beast represents a kingdom. The first beast was like a lion and
had wings of an eagle: it represented Babylon. God presented Babylon
as the king of the jungle (lion) and the king of the air (eagle). Babylon
was the greatest kingdom during the time of the prophesy, 560 BC. [1]

The second beast was like a bear, raised up on one of its sides with
three ribs in its mouth. The second kingdom was the Medo-Persian
Empire. The Medes were strong until the Persian Empire rose up and
defeated them, creating the largest empire in people and land. They
were defeated by the Persians — Cyrus the Great, 550 BC — and
combined forces to form a great army. [2]

A bear's power comes from its claws. The bear was raised up on
one side, indicating the Persian army was the strength of this kingdom. The bear was told: *"Get up and eat your fill of flesh."* The Medo-
Persians eventually conquered Babylon, as well as the Lydian and
Egyptian empires. [3]

The third was like a leopard with four wings, four heads, and authority to rule. This third kingdom was the Greek Empire and Alexander the Great. The leopard matches the speed at which the Greek army moved in battle, and the four wings and four heads represent the four generals that were left to rule after Alexander died at the age of 32. Lysimachus (who took Thrace and Bithynia), Cassander (who took Greece and Macedon), Seleucus (who took Babylonia and Syria) and Ptolemy (who took Palestine, Egypt, and Arabia). [4]

God confirms this prophecy even further later in Daniel chapter 8:

> "He said: 'I am going to tell you what will happen later in the time of wrath, because the vision concerns the appointed time of the end. The two-horned ram that you saw represents the kings of Media and Persia. The shaggy goat is the king of **Greece**, and the large horn between his eyes is the first king. The four horns that replaced the one that was broken off represent four kingdoms that will emerge from his nation but will not have the same power.'" (Dan. 8:19-22)

The fourth beast (Dan. 7:7) was "terrifying and frightening and very powerful. It had large iron teeth;" it crushed, devoured and trampled victims; it had ten horns. From a logical progression in history, this fourth beast can be none other than the **Roman empire** and the description that God gave Daniel describes it very well. The ten horns represent "ten kings who will come from this kingdom" (Dan. 7:24).

God repeated and confirmed between 600-560 BC the two prophecies on the coming kingdoms. He was in control and used the Medo-Persians to bring the downfall of Babylon. He raised up Alexander the Great and the Greeks destroyed the Medo-Persians (334-323 BC). The Romans came into power and their remnants may very well be the ten horns of today.

God is omniscient and reveals His power so that we may believe and trust in Him. And the one-time dreams came true and became reported and recorded history. God speaks truth, even before it is!

And just as God foretold of the coming everlasting Kingdom founded in Jesus Christ, we turn the pages of Holy Writ and advancing prophecy to New Testament dreams…

10. JOSEPH'S NEW TESTAMENT DREAMS

Matthew recorded the most all-time shell-shocking stories: God would come in the form of a baby. This would fulfill a 700-year-old prophecy, for Isaiah had prophesied: *"Therefore the Lord himself will give you a sign: The virgin will be with child and will give birth to a son, and will call him Immanuel"* (Isa. 7:14). Now, we take Him for granted: Of course, *God would come to be with us!*

But we forget **He is GOD!**

Here was the setting: Mary was pledged to marry Joseph but *"she was found to be with child through the Holy Spirit…. Joseph…was a righteous man and did not want to expose her to public disgrace; he had in mind to divorce her quietly."* God had to work for the good of Joseph, Mary and us and so *"an **angel of the Lord appeared to him in a dream** and said, 'Joseph son of David, do not be afraid to take Mary home as your wife, because what is conceived in her is from the Holy Spirit. She will give birth to a son, and you are to give him the name Jesus, because he will save his people from their sins.'*

"All this took place to fulfill what the Lord had said through the prophet: 'The virgin will be with child and will give birth to a son, and they will call him 'Immanuel'—which means, 'God with us.'

"When Joseph woke up, he did what the angel of the Lord had commanded him and took Mary home as his wife. But he had no union with her until she gave birth to a son. And he gave him the name Jesus." (Mt. 1:20-25)

God is always causing *"everything to work together for the good of those who love God and are called according to his purpose for them"* (Rom. 8:28). I call it a *"ping"* — a moment in time when God moves in the spiritual realm through people, circumstances, and an outpouring of His Love to touch you in a tangible way. In this particular *"ping,"* God sent an angel of the Lord to appear to Joseph. God had a powerful plan in play and Joseph was a big part of the plan. Joseph had to accompany Mary (and Jesus) to Bethlehem as she couldn't do that alone.

And God sent another dream to Joseph: *"When they had gone, an **angel of the Lord appeared to Joseph in a dream**. 'Get up,' he said, 'take the child and his mother and escape to Egypt. Stay there until I tell you, for Herod is going to search for the child to kill him.' So he got up, took the child and his mother during the night and left for Egypt, where he stayed until the death of Herod"* (Mt. 2:13-15). Joseph was needed to protect the newborn baby Jesus and Mary from assassins.

God used dreams to **protect and guide** Joseph, Mary, and Jesus. The lesson for us: God used dreams in the Old Testament as well as in the New Testament. God is the same, yesterday, today, and tomorrow. God used dreams in the past and He will give us dreams for today. Stay tuned to His dream broadcast!

One final dream that we'll cover was given to one of history's greatest leaders, Alexander the Great. This final dream is covered in a surprise twist: not from the pages of Holy Writ but from the annals of history.

11. ALEXANDER'S DREAM AS REPORTED BY JOSEPHUS

Alexander the Great was one of the greatest generals of history; tutored by the philosopher Aristotle until the age of 16. Alexander succeeded the throne at the age of 20 (336 BC), when his father Phillip was assassinated. He shrewdly eliminated all potential rivals. He then put down the revolts in all areas of his empire. And with each victory, Alexander added to his army and became even greater.

In 333 BC with approximately 40,000 foot soldiers and 5,000 cavalry, Alexander began his campaign against the Persian Empire. It was legendarily bold: Alexander threw a spear into Asian soil and proclaimed that he accepted Asia as **a gift from the gods**. By 331 BC Alexander gained victory over the Persians and Darius, Syria, then undertook a seven-month siege of Tyre and a two-month siege of Gaza. [5]

Flavius Josephus shares a unique story in his "Antiquities of the Jews": "When the seven months of the siege of Tyre were over, and the two months of the siege of Gaza... Alexander made haste to go up to Jerusalem; and **Jaddua the high priest**, when he heard that, was in agony, and under terror... the king was displeased at his foregoing disobedience. He therefore ordained that the people should make supplications, and join him in offering sacrifice to God, whom he besought to protect that nation, and to deliver them from the perils that were coming upon them; whereupon **God warned him in a dream... that he should take courage, and adorn the city, and open the gates; that the rest should appear in white garments, but that he and the priests should meet the king in the habit proper to their order, without the dread of any ill consequences, which the providence of God would prevent.** Upon which, when he rose from his sleep, he greatly rejoiced, and declared to all the warning he had received from God. **According to which dream he acted entirely,** and so waited for the coming of the king.

"And when he understood that he was not far from the city, he went out in procession, with the priests and the multitude of the citizens... Alexander, when he saw the multitude at a distance, in white garments, while the priests stood clothed with fine linen, and the high priest in purple and scarlet clothing, with his mitre on his head, having the golden plate whereon the name of God was engraved, he approached by himself, and adored that name, and first saluted the high priests. The Jews also did all together, with one voice, salute Alexander... whereupon the kings of Syria and the rest were surprised at what Alexander had done, and supposed him disordered in his mind. However, Parmenio (his trusted general) alone went up to him, and asked him how it came to pass that, when all others adored him, he should adore the high priest of the Jews?

"To whom he replied, 'I did not adore him, but that God who hath honored him with his high priesthood: for **I saw this very person in a dream**, in this very habit, when I was at Dios in Macedonia, who, when I was considering with myself how I might obtain the dominion of Asia, exhorted me to make no delay, but boldly to pass over the sea thither, for that he would conduct my army, and would give me the dominion over the Persians; whence it is that, having seen no other in that habit, and now seeing this person in it, and remembering that vision, and the exhortation which I had in my dream, I believe that I bring this army under the Divine conduct, and shall therewith conquer Darius, and destroy the power of the Persians, and that all things will succeed according to what is in my own mind.'

"And when he had said this to Parmenio, and had given the high priest his right hand, the priests ran along by him, and he came into the city. And when he went up into the temple, he offered sacrifice to God, according to the high priest's direction, and magnificently treated both the high priest and the priests.

"And when the **Book of Daniel** was showed him wherein **Daniel declared that one of the Greeks should destroy the empire of the Persians, he supposed that himself was the person intended.** And as he was then glad, he...bid them ask what favors they pleased of him; whereupon the high priest desired that they might enjoy the laws of their forefathers, and might pay no tribute on the seventh year. He granted all they desired." [6]

Surely the book Jaddua showed Alexander the Great was the Biblical book of Daniel, written in 530 BC. Alexander is living in the year 330 BC. God gave prophecy to Daniel about a king who was not living yet. Astounding! Here is the specific Scripture that inspired Alexander the Great:

> *"In the third year of King Belshazzar's reign, I, Daniel, had a vision, after the one that had already appeared to me...I looked up, and there before me was a ram with two horns [Medo-Persians], standing beside the canal, and the horns were long. One of the horns was longer than the other but grew up later [Persians]. I watched the ram as he charged toward the west and the north and the south. No animal could stand against him, and none could rescue from his power. He did as he pleased and became great.*
>
> *"As I was thinking about this, suddenly a* **goat with a prominent horn between his eyes came from the west, crossing the whole earth without touching the ground.** *He came toward the two-horned ram I had seen standing beside the canal and charged at him in great rage. I saw him attack the ram furiously, striking the ram and shattering his two horns. The ram was powerless to stand against him; the goat knocked him to the ground and trampled on him, and none could rescue the ram from his power. The goat became very great, but at the height of his power his large horn was broken off, and in its place four prominent horns grew up toward the four winds of heaven.*
>
> *"And I heard a man's voice from the Ulai calling,* **'Gabriel, tell this man the meaning of the vision.'** *As he came near the place where I was standing, I was terrified and fell prostrate. 'Son of man,' he said to me, 'understand that the vision concerns the time of the end.'*
>
> *"While he was speaking to me, I (Daniel) was in a* **deep**

sleep (dream), with my face to the ground. Then he touched me and raised me to my feet. He said: 'I (Gabriel) am going to tell you what will happen later in the time of wrath, because the vision concerns the appointed time of the end. The two-horned ram that you saw represents the kings of Media and Persia. **The shaggy goat is the king of Greece, and the large horn between his eyes is the first king.** *The four horns that replaced the one that was broken off represent four kingdoms that will emerge from his nation but will not have the same power.'"* (Dan. 8:5-22)

God used two dreams — one given to Alexander the Great, and one to Jaddua, the high priest — to **"ping"** the world. Can you just see Omniscient God jumping up and down, waving His arms and saying, **"I AM the great I AM. Trust me!"** God can use dreams, donkeys, and even me to write this and **"ping"** you! Start dreaming!

CONCLUSION

As we conclude this vital chapter on Biblical dreams we see many lessons we may apply to our dreams:

* Dreams are not only for "holy people" but for all, even you and me!
* God gives sustaining prophecies to give you hope until His plan comes to pass. Cling to His dreams!
* God works even when we are not aware of it to protect us.
* Once you "awaken" to interpreting your own dreams, you'll be gifted to also help others.
* Interpretation is from God.
* God speaks in symbols you'll be familiar with and will make sense to you.
* Dreams and visions are very intimate, personal communication. It's a special secret language spoken between you and the God you

39

love. Spend time getting to know Him in His Word!

* Some advanced dreams will only be revealed to you if you're tuned into God's wavelength.
* Dreams are part of God's eternal plan: Yes, it's to bless you in your life specifically but it's also to fulfill His "Bigger Picture" prophecy for all people and all time. How exciting!
* Don't be afraid of being afraid: Like Gideon, ask God for more confirmation if you need it or a spiritual friend as a "backup." God will meet you at your fears. He'll happily grow your faith! Just ask.
* Last, God not only validated His prophecies by cross-referencing Himself across Scripture but also by cross-checking Himself in history.

God is Author and Finisher of all dreams: from conception in your mind to fulfillment in our world. He used prophetic dreams to establish His Kingdom Come in Jesus Christ. And He continues to author dreams in you for all people today!

---

[1] Stamp, Donald C. 2003 *Life in the Spirit Study Bible*. Grand Rapids, Michigan, USA, Zondervan.

[2] Achaemenid Empire. In *Wikipedia*. Retrieved April 24, 2015, from http://en.wikipedia.org/wiki/Achaemenid_Empire

[3] Stamp

[4] Stamp

[5] Alexander the Great. In *Wikipedia*. Retrieved April 24, 2015, from http://en.wikipedia.org/wiki/Alexander_the_Great

[6] Josephus, Flavius (author) & Whitson, William (translator). 1960. *The Complete Works of Josephus*. Kregel Publications.

Figure 1. Nebuchadnezzar Statue

Figure 2. Honolulu Stadium

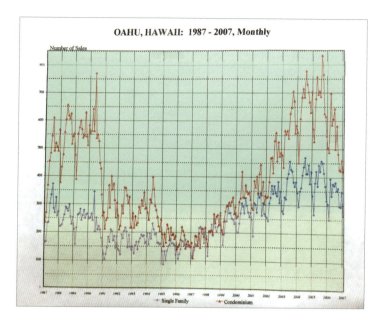

Figure 3. Top of the Real Estate Market

Figure 4. Ninja Centipede

Figure 5. Darrick and Missy

Figure 6. Darrick and Missy, New Home

Figure 7. Les Charmaines

Figure 8. Christ Redeemer

Figure 9. Kauluwela field

Figure 10. Family

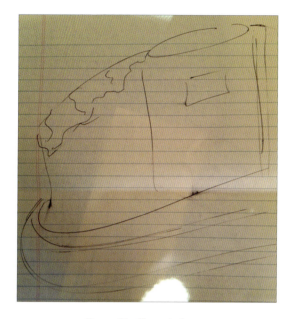

Figure 11. Daven's dream

Figure 12. Valley Bible

Figure 13. Bread

Figure 14. Dae's work

Figure 15. Donna & Dad

Figure 16. Jason and Donna

Figure 17. Grandpa, Grandma and Jason

Figure 18. Dad 1946

Figure 19. Alexander and Mildred Brostek

Figure 20. Mildred Brostek 1937

Figure 21. Peter and Ritsuko 1ˢᵗ meeting

Figure 22. Peter and Ritzi

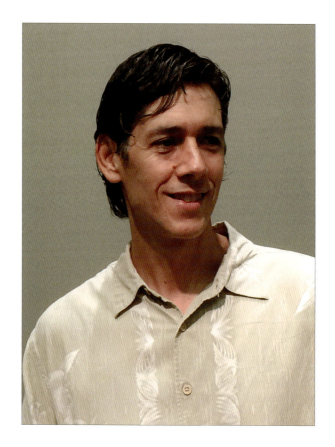

Figure 23. Dr. Jordan Seng

Figure 24. John and Pat Rodgers

Figure 25. Kaola Way to Booth Park

3

GOD'S DREAM TOOLKIT

"When I was a young child,
I used to have dreams in the night
that would come true the next day
or the following week.
Sometimes the things I dreamed about seemed positive,
but sometimes they were negative or scary,
and it used to freak me out because I didn't know what
was going on."
~ Dr. Jordan Seng, Senior Pastor,
Bluewater Mission Church

GOD'S LANGUAGE BARRIERS

My first experience living with a different language was at **Hawaii Cedar Church**, a congregation with many first-generation Koreans. Many came to Hawaii between 1960 and 1980. In fact, they're still arriving; there may be as many as 30,000 first-generation Koreans in Hawaii today. They speak broken English. I say this without prejudice; in fact, I have a Korean daughter-in-law and a future Korean son-in-law. Koreans are very honorable and have adapted well to America, but they're sometimes hard to understand. More importantly, it's hard to comprehend the way they see life because of their unique culture and paradigms.

The Koreans have a similar conversational manner to the Chinese: straight forward and hot, like *kim chee* (Korean spicy pickled vegetables). Perhaps one of the greatest keys in understanding Koreans was this: In the past century, Koreans suffered much during the Japanese occupation (1910-1941), WWII, and the Korean War.

Prior to and during WWII, Japan conscripted as many as five million Korean men for slave labor: "Of the 5,400,000 Koreans conscripted, about 670,000 were taken to mainland Japan...for civilian labor.... Those who were brought to Japan were often forced to work under appalling and dangerous conditions. The total deaths of Korean forced laborers in Korea and Manchuria is estimated to be between 270,000 and 810,000." [1]

Furthermore, when the Communist regime set up in North Korea after the Korean War, many families were split up. Sons lost fathers, mothers lost daughters, and brothers lost sisters. No wonder Korean war dramas today still depict the enemy as Japanese!

The first-generation Koreans who came to Hawaii Cedar Church had a lot of "baggage," history I cannot even begin to comprehend. So when God first called Diana and I to the church, I had a few communication barriers:

1. The Korean language
2. Korean history & culture
3. The intrinsic pain of the Koreans
4. Korean dislike of the Japanese

As you may now understand, open communication between our Korean congregation and Japanese me was difficult. On the one hand, I served as pastor and Koreans honor pastors. Also, they opened their church to the poor and fed them lunch after service, however, they didn't treat them well. They locked their refrigerators and served themselves better food than they served the poor. (Many of us treat the poor the same.) My challenge: As I was called by God, **how could I build bridges and blast barriers?**

BUSTING LANGUAGE BARRIERS

If I didn't comprehend the *"language of God,"* I would have left long before God could get me started. God's language is **AGAPE**. God loves all, including Koreans, and He wanted me to love and serve them. God wanted me to be influenced by their love for the poor, not dissuaded by their disservice. I may not speak Korean, but I can (with God's help) speak Agape, which all people understand. The lesson here: **Agape is the foundational language for understanding God, people, and dreams.**

My second barrier was the Korean culture and history. As I look at our shared past through their eyes, I can see why they may react a certain way. And I gain a greater vision: How to love them beyond our humanity. Likewise, God also has a His-story to help us understand His perspective; one He has written and given to us in the Bible. **And as I view events through His eyes, I understand dreams better. This helps to persist in His calling, beyond a limited line of vision.**

The third "language" barrier was to understand the Koreans' pain. I came to overlook their seeming insensitivity to the poor. Similarly, God endured pain; in fact, Jesus suffered the greatest pain. And Father God had so much pain looking upon His Son on the cross that He had to avert His eyes for an instant. Pain and suffering are part of God's language for living a full life in our fallen world. We, like Christ, will suffer for love. Therefore, dreams have this as a foundational reference point: **Suffering is not all bad.**

The fourth "language" barrier was Korean dislike of the Japanese. I came to realize that Koreans might dislike Japan as a nation but still love a Japanese individual. The application: **God dislikes sin, yet loves the sinner.** Once you and I get that, we may understand God's dreams. Otherwise, sin prevents me from clearly interpreting dreams and becomes a stronghold. (Bonus: On strongholds, read Ed Silvoso's, "That None Should Perish," Chapter 4). Dreams place a high value on people, even sinners.

If we are to understand the language of God in dreams or in any form, we must break down all barriers to understanding. I learned this through my Korean church family: That it's not simply about learning Korean language but about learning everything about Korean people. The same is to be applied with all people of all races, faiths, backgrounds, socio-economic statuses and stations...

AGAPE: "MY SHEEP KNOW MY VOICE"

Jesus said: "My *sheep know me... My sheep listen to my voice; I know them, and they follow me*" (Jn. 10:14, 27). Jesus is teaching a truth we all aim for but none has yet fully accomplished: A perfect connection with the Father, Son, and Holy Spirit. We continually aspire to hear His voice and obey.

Ironically, I have an easier time understanding the Koreans (they surround me) than I do God. After 20 years, I'm more able to hear my main mission from God, but what's difficult is hearing His monthly, weekly, and even daily assignments.

Jesus said: "Be **perfect**, *therefore as your heavenly Father is* **perfect**" (Mt. 5:48). Perfection is impossible, but Agape is more than possible and that's what Jesus is talking about: Having perfect **Agape** for God and others. One path to perfection is what Jesus told Peter: "Keep on keeping on! Keep doing what I told you to do." And what is that? "**Feed my sheep.**" Share the Gospel with **Agape**.

DREAMS DIRECT US ON GOD'S PATH

Dreams help us to stay on target and adjust at critical crossroads. (By His grace He chooses His communication method for each of us. If you've noticed a consistent method, pay attention, He's talking to you!) And knowing God's communication tools de-mystifies His spiritual language. It's less far-fetched and more heart-to-heart, just as He intends it to be. A good place to start is to **believe God will speak to you in your primary mode of communication**. I love dreams because I enjoy sleeping! If you sleep and believe (just a little extra effort), you can hear from God. And you have a fresh chance every night!

I. GOD'S METHODS IN DREAMS:

A. USE OF PATTERNS

God uses patterns in the Bible. Birds are birds but they may also be a metaphor. The tip-off? When there's a pattern of repetition, you can be sure that God is saying something deeper.

And God can use anything as a metaphor. He can also create personifications, similes, allegories, and stories; even word pictures of things we don't know. God is the greatest storyteller! And symbols are an important part of God's dream language, so it behooves us to understand them.

Our starting point to understand God's dream language is the Bible. God stocks His Bible full of word pictures, images and metaphors. This is our textbook for "Dream 101" language. It's a foundation for our understanding as it helps interpret what He's telling us in the dreams He sends. If you still don't know, gather a group to pray and help you interpret.

Here is a list of a few foundational, Biblical symbols:

1. BIRDS

There are 93 Bible passages containing *"bird"* or *"birds."* Most are literal, however, here are a few bird Scriptures that are symbolic:

"The Lord said to him, 'Bring me a heifer, a goat and a ram, each three years old, along with a dove and a young pigeon.' Abram brought all these to him, cut them in two and arranged the halves opposite each other; the birds, however, he did not cut in half. Then **birds** *of prey came down on the carcasses, but Abram drove them away."* (Gen. 15: 9-11)

God revealed a negative vision: Abram was forced to drive away birds that came to steal God's sacrifice. Here, God was answering Abram's question, *"How will I know that I'll possess [the land]?"* God's answer: "I will do it"; pointing to Jesus as the fulfillment of His promise. However, the birds symbolized the evil that would try to pilfer that promise.

"As he was scattering the seed, some fell along the path, and the birds came and ate it up.... When anyone hears the message about the kingdom and does not understand it, the evil one comes and snatches away what was sown in his heart. This is the seed sown along the path." (Mt. 13:4, 19)

Jesus teaches that these birds represent the evil one who comes and snatches away what was sown in people's hearts. Now, don't put your pet birds down! Many passages value birds. **Context is key**. Birds are one of God's most common dream pictures.

2. YEAST

There are over 50 passages containing the term "yeast." Yeast is good; it makes dough rise and bread fluffy. We couldn't live (easily) without yeast. (Unless you're a rice person.) However, God chose yeast as a picture of sin and evil, one that pollutes:

"That same night they are to eat the meat roasted over the fire, along with bitter herbs, and bread made without yeast." (Ex. 12:8)

"Do not offer the blood of a sacrifice to me along with anything containing yeast." (Ex. 23:18)

"How is it you don't understand that I was not talking to you about bread? But be on your guard against the yeast of the Pharisees and Sadducees." (Mt. 16:11)

"Your boasting is not good. Don't you know that a little yeast works through the whole batch of dough?" (1 Cor. 5:6)

God decides on the good or evil meaning of a metaphor. The key to interpretation will be the **context** of your life within which He sends the dream.

3. BREAD

There are 255 passages containing *"bread."* Most depict bread as food, a life-giving staple. However, a few passages also provide a spiritual view of bread:

*"While they were eating, Jesus took **bread**, gave thanks and broke it, and gave it to his disciples, saying, 'Take and eat; this is my **body**.'"* (Mt. 26:26)

*"Give us each day our daily **bread**."* (Lk. 11:3)

*"Then Jesus declared, 'I am the **bread of life**. He who comes to me will never go hungry, and he who believes in me will never be thirsty.'"* (Jn. 6:35)

*"They devoted themselves to the apostles' teaching and to the fellow-ship, to the **breaking of bread** and to prayer."* (Acts 2:42)

A dream about bread is typically a good sign. God sent a "bread dream" to our son Daven regarding a house they were to purchase. (More details coming in Chapter 5.)

4. FIG TREE

The Bible also includes a common symbol of *"figs"* or *"the fig tree,"* representing Israel: *"The Lord, the God of Israel, says: 'Like these good figs, I regard as good the exiles from Judah, whom I sent away from this place to the land of the Babylonians. My eyes will watch over them for their good, and I will bring them back to this land….'"* (Jer. 24:5-6)

"'But like the poor figs, which are so bad they cannot be eaten,' says the Lord, 'so will I deal with Zedekiah king of Judah, his officials and the survivors from Jerusalem, whether they remain in this land or live in Egypt.'" (Jer. 24:8)

"When I found Israel, it was like finding grapes in the desert; when I saw your fathers, it was like seeing the early fruit on the fig tree." (Hos. 9:10)

The most important key for understanding dreams is **context** (more in Chapter 7); however, the whole picture is also important. Each individual dream is God's way of expressing a deeper relationship with you, therefore call out to Him for clarity; call out to Him for confirmation; call out to Him to guide your steps. Symbols — like birds, yeast, bread, fruit trees — give us a key to unlocking God's dreams. Another key to opening God's dream doors are actions.

B. USE OF ACTION WORDS/VERBS

* **Cupbearer** (Gen. 40): The notable action was the cupbearer *"put"* the cup in Pharaoh's hand, which was a good action. Pharaoh was blessed with wine.
* **Baker** (Gen. 40): Birds were *"eating"* the breadbasket on his head; a bad action. Although bread is normally good, Pharaoh didn't get the bread, the evil birds did.
* **Pharaoh's dream** (Gen. 41): Skinny cows *ate* the fat cows, again a bad action.
* **The goat** (Dan. 8): It **charged** the ram and **destroyed** it. Obviously negative.

Action words can help determine whether a dream is good or bad. The question to ask God: *What is **His** meaning for the action that He revealed in your dream? And then, as always: What does this dream mean in the context of what is going on around me?*

Another tool in God's dream kit is contrasting pictures:

C. USE OF CONTRAST

God loves great contrasts: hot vs. cold, "yes" vs. "no," and wise vs. foolish. Why? Because God knows that contrast makes an instant impression. It's easy to get! In Pharaoh's dream (Gen. 41) the contrast was in the cows and the grain: skinny vs. fat; and thin vs. healthy. Contrast helps us to see simple meaning. God also uses contrast as a tool of repetition and repetition is God turning the volume to full blast. God not only uses contrast with pictures but more deeply with concepts or principles:

CONTRASTING CONCEPTS

"The Lord Almighty says: 'Ask the priests what the law says: If a person carries consecrated meat in the fold of his garment, and that

fold touches some bread or stew, some wine, oil or other food, does it become consecrated?' The priests answered, 'No.' Then Haggai said, 'If a person defiled by contact with a dead body touches one of these things, does it become defiled?' 'Yes,' the priests replied, 'it becomes defiled.' Then Haggai said, 'So it is with this people and this nation in my sight,' declares the Lord. 'Whatever they do and whatever they offer there is defiled.'" (Hag. 2:11-14)

Here is a contrast of concepts: Touch does not necessarily consecrate a person to holiness but it can defile a person. Look for conceptual contrast in your dreams; a dream that seems senseless may become one with useful lessons.

Contrast is an easy tool for getting divine ideas across simply. Contrasting concepts takes it even deeper. It's more complicated but it's another tool God uses to communicate His ideas to our limited understanding. It's well worth the extra effort to strain your brain and gain God's greater vision for your life.

Another tool God uses, much to many people's surprise, are emotions. Many are shocked that God even uses fear...

D. USE OF EMOTIONS ~ FEAR

1. CULTURAL FEARS

God knows that fear has the power to get automatic attention. People who don't realize that God uses fear make the mistake of simply sloughing off the dream. *No!* You must know that sometimes God has to scare the "pants off of us"!

A good friend, Kent, knew God early in life but took a wrong turn. One day, as he was driving back from the North Shore after a drug buy, he decided to pull over, sit in the back seat and sample a substantial amount. He was struck by a vision: Satan pointed directly at him and said: *"You're mine!"* It scared him to death. Kent immediately started his journey back to God. That was over 30 years ago and today Kent is a strong Christian married to a stronger Christian wife. He reports, "It still give me the creeps even thinking about it!" God scared him straight.

God uses nightmares as a warning to get people back on the right track. Many people have told me about nightmares they've had when they were on drugs, like Kent, and the nightmares stopped when they stopped doing drugs. People might think drugs cause nightmares, however, I think God sends nightmares to get people to turn to Him. **Abimelech** (Gen. 20), **Pharaoh** (Gen. 41), and **Nebuchadnezzar** (Dan. 2 and 4) all had nightmares and were deeply disturbed. God used those bad dreams to guide them in their destiny as He worked for their good and for the good of Israel.

2. FEAR OF FALLING

How can one have the feeling of falling when one is sleeping? When I was young I had a recurring dream: I'm at Honolulu Stadium and after being chased by a Tyrannosaurus Rex, I climb to the top of the stadium walls and jump over to escape the Rex. (figure 2, page 42) I fell for a long time and then woke up. One thing is sure, the feeling was real. In my dream, I felt exactly the same feeling that I did when I ride the Pirates of the Caribbean and take that first dip (after the fireflies). It's only about a 25' fall, but I don't open my eyes; the feeling is too spooky. So I cannot ride high Ferris Wheels, and don't like any rides that "fall suddenly." The few times that I rode baby roller coasters, I endured my fears for my family's sake. I wouldn't sacrifice for you; I'm too scared of the feeling.

I've had many dreams of falling and the dream is as real as a real-life plunge. And in talking with others who've shared the same nightmare, it's very real. One urban legend is that if you don't wake up before you hit the ground, you'll die. A fool's tale.

But what does it mean?

How is it possible to be fast asleep and experience "falling"?

My one-track mind gives one explanation: **God**. Only God can create that feeling, even while we sleep. He wants us to know that He knows our fears and only by a relationship with Him will our fears be eliminated. God wants us to know He sends dreams and He can trigger fear, if necessary.

God uses the human palette of emotions to paint graphic pictures; and we get it! That's Dream 101. However, God may also up your dream level to "advanced" and take you to "Level: Heaven"!

E. USE OF HEAVENLY INSTRUMENTS

One of the all-time greatest dreams is one in which God uses divine instruments: angels, stars, a cross, even a picture of Heaven or a visit from Jesus Himself. Yes, it can happen! Expect it and pray for it!

Hal and Lana Jones are missionaries who head an organization called **Global Hope Network International**. They bring the "practical Gospel": Clean water systems, sanitation, disease prevention, home health, education for children and resources for sustainable family income generation. They also do village transformation, disaster relief, slavery prevention, and leadership training. All in Jesus' name!

While on a trip to Hawaii, Hal brought a missionary friend, Phillip, an Arab Christian living in Israel. I'd heard of Muslims having dreams or visions of Jesus, so I asked if he knew any. He confirmed that he personally knew of a number of cases. It was truly exciting to hear his first-hand reports.

A recent article in "BreakPoint" shares similar stories:

"David Garrison, a missions expert with the Southern Baptists, has written an amazing new book called 'A *Wind in the House of Islam*,' which describes an unprecedented movement of Muslims into the Christian faith over the last twenty years.

"Upon hearing the increasing stories of conversions recently in the Islamic world, David went on a journey of 250,000 miles to speak with Muslims in West Africa, North Africa, the Middle East, Central Asia, the Persian world, South Asia, and the Indo-Malaysia archipelago, asking them the fundamental question, **'What did God use to bring you to faith in Jesus Christ?'**

"His research uncovered that in the fourteen hundred years since Muhammad founded Islam, there have been 82 movements of Muslims turning to Christ. As a starting point, he defined **'movement'** as 1,000 Muslims receiving Christian baptism, a public statement of their faith in Christ.

"Now 82 movements in 1,400 years doesn't sound like a lot. But David Garrison points out an amazing fact—84% of those movements have started in just the last 20 years. There is indeed a new wind blowing!

"'We're seeing a moment in salvation history,' Garrison claims, 'that we've never seen before in the history of Christianity's interaction with the House of Islam.'

"In many cases, Garrison notes, the Lord is using **dreams and visions of Jesus Christ** to overcome old barriers and reach Muslim hearts. Those dreams are often followed up by a Christian who points the seeking to the gospel....

"When I asked Garrison why God might be giving more dreams to Muslims today, his answer was sobering: 'My fear,' he said, 'is that they may have been having **dreams and visions** for fourteen centuries, but there was no one there to tell them who Jesus was, no one there to give them a New Testament in their own language to share with them the good news that God loves Muslims.'" [2]

F. USE OF DIRECTIONS

The best Christian conference in the world is held in Hawaii hosted by **Hawaiian Islands Ministries** (HIM). HIM was founded by Dr. Dan and Pam Chun back when I had hair and was tearing up the world. They founded HIM in 1983 and held their first conference in 1985.

Their dream: "What if the world's best Christian communicators and teachers could come to speak regularly at a conference in Hawaii? What if all the Christian leaders could hear and be trained by them? What if local Christian churches from across denominations were impacted and renewal was sparked?" Our friend said, 'Not *what if* but *when.*' That moment, HIM took its first breath."

It is impossible to measure the eternal impact that HIM has had on my life. I attended my first HIM conference at the Ilikai Hotel in 1994. It was a supernatural experience. I started with an early surf session and happened to see Pastor Dan walking into the conference. I'd just heard Dr. Dobson on the radio sharing the same issue that was the theme at the conference. So I stopped Pastor Dan and asked what his planned comments were to be (I was a baby Christian and on fire). Dan was gracious. I've since apologized for my rude interruption. He doesn't remember it, or maybe he's just being nice (which he is).

At a recent HIM, **Dr. Jordan Seng** was teaching on the prophetic move of God, including dreams. He taught that **if we have a dream and we are in a car, boat, airplane, or on a road; God may be showing us life or mission direction. If you're going uphill, it indicates difficulty; downhill indicates ease.** Another divine clue! It helped Diana and I with a particularly odd dream that she had...[3]

DIANA'S DREAM

In her spare time, Diana takes a team of about eight women to Leahi Hospital to love on patients. Diana started by herself but God brought other women alongside her. They've been doing this every week for almost 10 years. They sing, dance, make them laugh, massage their backs, and pray for them, then they get down to business: They eat!

A few years ago, Diana had a dream: She was at Leahi Hospital escorting people dressed in long white robes to board buses. The dream shifted to the back of a limousine with two rows of seats facing each other. She was with another lady, seated in the same row. Between them were demons, human-looking with catlike facial features. The demons were attacking the other lady. Diana frantically tried to escape but she couldn't open the door. She was terrified but she didn't pray or call out to God. She just tried to flee.

Around the same time in our lives, **Pastor Francis Oda** shared about his church's intercessory team. Pastor Francis is an architect and every job is a ministry opportunity. Therefore, when he goes into the field, he activates the prayer team as his spiritual covering. Then, together, they see God move and work miracles. Well, if it's good for Pastor Francis, it's good for Pastor Jimmy!

So in Summer 2013, I asked Diana to pray about leading our intercessory prayer team. This was important as we didn't yet have one. Diana took time to hear from God and then gingerly took on the mantle. Now they pray before every service.

In looking back at Diana's linked dreams — of Leahi Hospital buses and then the limousine — she realized that God was telling her that she was spiritually weak. God had given her the responsibility to minister to souls, seen as escorting people onto a bus to heaven. She was strong while serving and doing *external* acts; God was pleased.

However, in her soul, Diana was still afraid of demons (a cultural thing that went way back for her). Even when she walked our dog before sunrise, she'd pray: "Oh, God, don't let me see any demons behind the trees!" In her limo dream, God showed Diana she needed to grow stronger in spirit.

That dream included multiple levels of communication from God: 1) who she was: fearful of demons; 2) a life journey: ministering to souls; 3) direction: to gain victory over her fear by growing strong in spirit. It was not initially obvious, which is why it's important to record dreams and be sure to look back. And keep pressing God for **His** interpretation. It will come.

Diana's dream was a perfect illustration and application of Dr. Jordan Seng's teaching: Transit and direction (going up or down). It's another clue for decoding divine dreams. Next: What type is it?

II. TYPES OF GOD-DREAMS

God has five main types of dreams: 1) lesson-teaching; 2) future-revealing; 3) warning; 4) character-revealing; and 5) simply "talk story." **All dreams are either authored by God or allowed by God.**

A. LESSONS

God is forever teaching us one of the greatest lessons we could ever learn: God is omniscient, all-knowing. In the book of Daniel, God proves it in a dream about future kingdoms. The ultimate application is that we may trust God completely: He knows and sees all. He sees you even in your worst depravity, when you're doing the worst of the worst. God knows it and still He loves you. **This is the "blessed assurance": That you and I may trust and rest in His unconditional love.**

(Aside: Nebuchadnezzar's dream covered four of the five types of dreams. It included lessons, future revelation, a warning, and it revealed his character. Many God-dreams contain multiple dream types, further providing irrefutable evidence that God knows all.)

Dreams quite often teach us lessons. Imagine, you slept in school and got scolded, now you sleep and get schooled by God! Isn't He awesome? Thank you, Lord!

B. REVEALING FUTURE

Many Biblical dreams provide prophecy. From the very beginning, Genesis, God revealed His future plans to His chosen people: Jacob had a dream *"in which he saw a stairway resting on the earth, with its top reaching to heaven, and the angels of God were ascending and descending"* (Gen. 28:12). God reiterated what He had already stated to Abram: He would give them the Promised Land.

God delivered and gave Israel its land. Today the nation of Israel occupies the very land that the Bible predicted would be given to them (Num. 34). God warned that they would be *"uprooted from the land"* if they did not fully obey Him (Deut. 28:63). God also predicted how He would bring them back:

> *"For I will take you out of the nations; I will gather you from all the countries and bring you back into your own land. I will sprinkle clean water on you, and you will be clean; I will cleanse you from all your impurities and from all your idols. I will give you a new heart and put a new spirit in you; I will remove from you your heart of stone and give you a heart of flesh. And I will put my Spirit in you and move you to follow my decrees and be careful to keep my laws. You will live in the land I gave your forefathers; you will be my people, and I will be your God." (Ez. 36:24-28)*

God returned His people back to their Israel after World War II in 1948. That was over 3,500 years after His prophecy to Jacob! And over 2,500 years after Ezekiel's prophecy! And almost 2,000 years after Israel was destroyed by the Roman general, Titus, in 70 AD. This is only one example of many, many more prophecies God gave through dreams!

C. WARNINGS, CORRECTIONS, DANGER AHEAD

In life, we often wander (or fall) off-track. God knows what's best for us and doesn't allow us to get too far off course without correction. One way He does so is through dreams that either warn us or warn others who will get the message to us.

God warned Abimelech through a dream so he wouldn't take Sarah as his wife (Gen. 20). Even though Abraham had lied about Sarah being his sister (a half-truth is a lie), God still protected Abraham and Sarah. God was protecting the future of the nation of Israel. God always protects His global plan.

So far, through dreams, we see that God is concerned with teaching lessons, showing the future, guiding through warnings, but He is most concerned about our character...

D. REVEALING CHARACTER

Character is who we are when only God is watching. He can reveal our true nature to us through dreams, if we have eyes to see it. We may be asleep but He wants us to know that He does not sleep and He knows all our frailties.

Men ask what their dreams mean when it's about sex. Answer: God is showing them what's on their minds. And for those who have dreams about doing drugs, God is showing what you're craving. If you have dreams about hitting the jackpot in Vegas or making a killing on Wall Street, God is probably not showing you the future. It's more likely that He's revealing what is on your mind: money.

There is no condemnation or judgment, I'm only sharing what God is doing in dreams. (I've had my share of correction.) It may be difficult to make sense of different dreams. **The Bible provides a basic foundation, however, only a deep relationship with Him reveals all.**

Christians who have a personal relationship with God should be able to go to Him and get interpretation. When in doubt, gather together *"for where two or three gather together in* **My name**, *there am I with them."* Jesus teaches that when we gather with a desire to hear from Him, He is there. With dreams, God will interpret through someone in the group. If not, find another group.

E. GOD LOVES TO "TALK STORY"

Most of our dreams are God simply talking story with us. Nothing major or critical; He just wants us to know that He loves us and wants to spend time with us. In the Old Testament, all of the dreams were of extreme importance: God was birthing Israel and developing the lineage of Jesus Christ. Today, His Kingdom has been established on earth, so God takes greater liberty with us in our dreams.

For us, we receive lessons, warnings, future revelation, and a glimpse of our character. However, I think God enjoys "talking story" the most. Of course, this is just my opinion; I don't have any Bible to back it up. I came to this conclusion through most of my dreams, which are "talk story" variety.

Here are a few "talk story" dreams recently recorded in my dream journal (no laughing):

9/7/14: At a sushi restaurant, the waitress doesn't want to take our order. I go to the hostess, whom I know. She brings us chow fun noodles. I still want to order sushi. (Maybe God is telling me I'm stubborn.)

9/5/14: I'm a secret agent, like 007; but my cell phone cannot turn off. Someone tries to help but instead they steal my battery.

5/30/14: I'm playing basketball and making long shots. Shifts to golf: I'm walking through the course, seems like an industrial area. I join a group with 3 golfers; we move ahead but cannot find other group.

1/23/14: Our dog, Piko, is hiding in a bus luggage compartment. I try to entice him out. Snow outside?

Allow me to stop while I'm ahead. (I'm sure you've had silly dreams too.) I only remembered certain scenes, but I journal only what I remember, which is why it's disjointed. These seem to have no lesson, warning, or correction. Some may read this and say they cannot be from God. Scientists tell us that our minds make them up or are simply processing the day's events.

However, what if God *is* talking story? Aren't they hilarious? Can you hear Him laughing? What if God was joking about my dog in a bus compartment, and I try to call him: "Here, Piko, come!" There's snow outside and God is sitting there watching it all go down. It's pretty cool to hang out with God. And when I realize He likes hanging out too, my relationship with Him deepens. That's HUGE!

CONCLUSION

As we conclude this chapter on God's dream toolkit we've covered quite a few tools:

First and foremost, God's language of Agape is universally understood and used throughout dreams; use it as the filter to help interpret your dreams. Agape is always the foundation. Learn the sound of the Shepherd's voice and then you'll be able to understand Him fluently when He speaks.

Second, God's methods include the use of patterns (symbols), action words, contrast, emotions (even fear!), heavenly beings, and even directions. Be aware of them all as you add to your Biblically-based "Dream 101" textbook.

Third, God-dreams can be organized in five types: lessons, prophecies, warnings, character-revealing, and talking story. All dreams are either authored or allowed by God. What is He saying to you?

And the greatest takeaway: Dreams must be understood in the context of God's language of **Agape**.

---

[1] Korea Under Japanese Rule. In *Wikipedia*. Retrieved April 24, 2015, from http://en.wikipedia.org/wiki/Korea_under_Japanese_rule

[2] Stonestreet, John. *"Muslims Dreaming of Jesus, A Wind in the House of Islam."* <http://www.breakpoint.org/bpcommentaries/entry/13/24501> n.p. February 10, 2014 5:30 A.M. Web 24, April, 2015

[3] Seng, Jordan. 2013. *Miracle Work: A Down-to-Earth Guide to Supernatural Ministries.* Downers Grove, IL. InterVarsity Press.

4

A FEW OF MY FAVORITE DREAMS

GOD SPEAKS WHEN WE'RE FAST ASLEEP?

The Bible clearly says that God communicates with people via dreams; however, I still wondered whether that applied to us today. *Might God really speak to me?*

Yet God did exactly that, speaking to my heart early in my walk with Him. Only God could have saved my life when I drove home totally bombed. After the accident, I looked at both the condition of the car and my body, and I KNOW without a doubt that God was there. (I don't argue with fools who say, "There's no God." No time for that. Better to love them and talk about the sun and moon, art, and the 49ers. Way more fun!)

My earliest instructions from God had to do with helping others, doing something, or going somewhere. He often communicated through circumstances — a need became obvious and I had the means, opportunity, or connections to meet it. Typically I would wait until the feeling grew stronger; or if I couldn't get it out of my mind (no matter how much I whacked my head). Discernment was knowing the needs that disappeared quickly were not instructions from God.

In this chapter, I share some of my favorite dreams.

GOD DIRECTS THOSE SEEKING DIRECTION

One of the first dreams I had was laying out a fleece to gain Godly confirmation. I prayed: "**God if You want me to do 'WHATEVER,' give me a dream about 'SOMETHING.'**" The "WHATEVER" was my situation. The "SOMETHING" was a specific thing. That way, if my dreams lined up with my "something," I could be sure God had answered. My desire was "Lord, what do You want?"

I shared earlier about asking God for a dreams. A key verse that guides us: "*In his heart a man plans his course, but the **Lord determines his steps**" (Prov. 16:9). The Lord guides those who want to serve Him. We plan things to the best of our ability, however, the Lord tells us when to turn, slow down, go faster, jump, or look up. Thankfully, God's step-by-step directions saved our company in global disaster.

TOP OF THE REAL ESTATE MARKET

A business' best dream is for a "hot market": When customers don't ask "What's the price?" They just buy, buy, buy! It can happen in any trade — stock market, restaurants, hotel industry or real estate.

In 2005, the real estate market was not just hot, it was molten, like lava. It happened due to an oversight by our government—the President, Congress, U.S. Treasury, and the Federal Reserve. They encouraged low interest rates and loosened laws and rules for purchasers to qualify for homeownership. And in doing so, they opened home ownership to many who were not qualified.

Construction boomed in Hawaii. Luxury condos and luxury hotels, big and mid-sized projects, housing subdivisions, commercial projects were all "molten." Most major subcontractors were turning away projects while adding better margins to projects. Our company, A-1 A-Lectrician, was no exception. The whole industry fought for staff: administrative, engineering, project management, field supervisors, and more. Companies offered higher pay to anyone willing to switch firms.

The greatest challenge was to decide which jobs to go after: Projects with more profit? Or projects with less risk? Projects with stronger contractors and developers? Or do we want more condos: luxury, market or affordable? You could never be sure which projects would move ahead and which would die. If you secured early entry into a project that died six months later, you would "inherit the wind." Our constant question at that time: *"Lord, which jobs are the ones to secure?"*

On **Saturday, August 27, 2005**, God sent a dream in three parts:

"Sat. Night – Dream (1) Latin Singer (Gloria Estefan) selling property (shack) on beach $5-7 Mill. (2) Friend selling townhse but had leased out front area to neighbor. (3) Mike/Paul – selling home. Long house—running thru hse—hitting walls."

I wrote what I believed God was telling me: "**End of Real Estate Bubble**."

The next weekend, Surfing the Nations (STN) was having a board meeting in an eight-bedroom Waialua beachhouse. God loved STN's ministry and it seemed impossible to separate us: the Yamadas, the Bauers, STN, our construction business (which was helping STN), and God. Our children, Daven and Lisa, had gone on STN missions. And I was doing weekly Bible studies at STN.

So the timing of the dreams, just prior to the three-day STN Board Retreat, was significant. God was revealing the importance of STN in the next phase of my life. And the purpose of the retreat was to refine mission and vision statements, as well as to look at overall organizational structure.

Over the next few weeks, I spent time processing A-1's marketing strategy in light of God's dreams. In construction there are always booms and busts. But, like life itself, while everyone knows something bad is around the corner, very few change plans to adapt. It's difficult as no one knows when the end will come. Most think, *Tomorrow!* The worst thing is to be 70-80% finished on a project that slams to a stop because of weak sales or buyer pull out. *Can we cover our construction costs and complete the project?* We can never know how solid the banks are and whether they will continue funding the project.

By mid-September, I decided to take action as God had revealed a real estate bust. Our strategy was to raise prices on luxury condos and luxury hotels. We had less work but I felt better securing projects with lower margins that wouldn't bust. It also allowed our competitors to secure all the work they could handle. If good times continued, we could secure more profitable work after our competitors were filled up. With that said, there was also a risk that the boom would end with A-1 **not** securing enough projects to go forward. But life is a risk, and we take the best calculated one. (figure 3, page 43)

By the next summer (2006), a large military project came to bid. Most major electrical contractors were filled up. We secured that project and with very good profit margins; in fact, the best ever for our company. The Hand of God had guided us to a large project that started in late 2007, which took us all the way through the devastating subprime disaster that wiped out so many projects and so many businesses. A-1 had its best three years during the global meltdown of 2008, 2009, and 2010.

Allow me to emphasize: We're not better, smarter, or more efficient than others in the business world, but **God had guided us through the period**. Our success was by *His* grace.

More importantly, that project provided my son Jason the experience he needed to become president of our firm. He too saw God's Hand throughout this challenging time. And we were all grateful for God's life-giving (and company-saving) dreams.

GOD'S HAND AT THE PROJECT BLESSING

At the ground blessing ceremony for the project, a large tent had been set up. Dignitaries were in attendance and **Kahu (Pastor) Kordell Kekoa** was on hand to officiate the blessing. The day was sunny, with no clouds overhead, and no wind; all was serenely calm. Kahu started to pray and spoke about God and the "wind." As soon as he said the word, "wind," a gentle breeze began to blow through the tent. Kahu went on and spoke of "rain." As soon as he said, "rain," a light drizzle began to fall. It was like music to those who recognized God was there.

After the ceremony, Jason busted into my office: "Dad, you should have seen what happened!" Our General Foreman, **Art Aoki**, burst in, looking like he had seen the face of God. Art confirmed exactly what Jason had experienced. God had moved and we all expected to see His Hand on this project.

YET ANOTHER MIRACLE

The project started and it needed to "come out of the ground." The General Contractor had to dig down, about 40 feet or so, and secure the foundation by pouring all the concrete walls to rise from the ground. Then the steel structure could be added, and they could secure the building so water would not be a problem. However, the location had a lot of water runoff from rains in the mountains. It would easily delay construction for months as the worst thing is to build in mud.

God's Hand moved: It turned out to be one of the driest periods for that area in years, allowing the General Contractor to "come out of the ground" in record time. The rest of the job had its share of issues, but for God's practical purpose, all went smoothly. Typically, large projects have construction delays that extend the construction period. This one ended up months ahead of schedule. Go God!

INTERLUDE

"In the last days, God says, I will pour out my Spirit on all people. Your sons and daughters will prophesy, your young men will see visions, your old men will dream dreams." (Acts 2:17)

Since we are living in the Last Days, God is flooding His people with dreams and visions. *All* can hear from God and *anyone* can be used by God. Just as a TV has a receiver, we need to tune our receivers to God's signal. God wants to use you. Get in the game! Stand up and say, "Here I am, Lord, use me! I'll do anything You want because I know You'll help me accomplish what You give me to do."

Also, allow me to add that I am not exaggerating or even lying "small kind." God doesn't need my help. He's bigger than that: He created the universe, spoke and there was light. He doesn't need light to create (like we do) and He certainly doesn't need me to make up stories about how great He is. However I accept the risk that you might think I'm drawing attention to myself. But I do this so you might believe that God can speak to you through dreams and visions or otherwise. I'll take the hit if you think I'm boasting; so what, I'm already wretched in God's sight. How can it get worse?

However, if you believe and start on God's dream journey, God will show up! You'll get excited to dream and to remember the dreams. Ultimately, you'll grow in a greater relationship with our great God.

THE COMING ECONOMIC TIDAL WAVE

In early 2007, I had three separate dreams. Here's the entry from my dream journal. (Note: If I had not kept a "Dream Journal," I might not have been able to tie the three dreams together as they were spaced out in time. Without notes, the brain forgets what is heard or seen. Example: What did your pastor preach last Sunday? Or two Sundays ago? *Hmm…* I prove my point and rest my case!)

Jan. 7, 2008: "Huge tidal wave coming—On high mountain ridge. Maybe 100 feet up. In concrete building. Feel like something is coming @ ocean—why am I there? See horses moving away from ocean. People mulling around (on sand). Eventually see tide retreating, so I know Tidal Wave coming."

I write my interpretation from God at the end: *"Economic Tidal Wave?"*

Feb. 20, 2008: @ Beach—looks like Ala Moana—big surf 8-10 feet. Scene shifts to big surf outside—boat (15') with girl in front and guy, gets towed in (like a Coast Guard rescue).

Feb. 27, 2008: Out surfing—50-foot swell–paddled over. Waiting for good wave—wave didn't break, water was shallow, fins touched reef.

After the second and third dreams, I realized something was about to happen economically. Then, **BANG!** On March 14, 2008, the news hit: The Bear Stearns Bailout. Something was up.

I was unable to do anything about projects that we were hoping to secure as most of our larger projects take four to six months to secure. The only thing that I could do was to get our company ready, both emotionally and mentally. Naturally, those who are strong in Spirit are easier to get prepared and pumped. A-1 called two communication meetings — one in Honolulu (April 18) and another on the Big Island (April 19) — to roll out the "Joseph Plan."

In Summer 2008, the subprime mortgage crisis hit and by September 15, Lehman Brothers went bankrupt. For the next year, the financial market tanked; many wondered if the banks were even going to make it. For our firm, God had guided and provided from the initial dream on August 27, 2005. He had secured enough work to sustain us through the recession. Thank you, Lord!

God also gave advance warning early in 2008 so A-1 could batten down the hatches and implement our "Joseph Plan" for economic survival. Joseph had saved 20% of the grain in Egypt to prepare for the forewarned famine. He did so for seven years. We followed that Biblical model of saving versus the worldly model of consumption. Our people adapted and we lived to fight another day.

CAN GOD USE A NINJA CENTIPEDE?

(Disclaimer: I've already shared this briefly in this book and in greater detail in an earlier book, so I'll simply hit the highlights here as it's relevant to the economic crisis.)

Summer 2008 was a global celebration in the China Olympics. On **Monday, August 25**, God sent a Ninja centipede to bite me while I was sleeping. I felt a sharp, intense pain and immediately sprang up, and threw the blankets off to see...*nothing?!* Diana woke up and helped search for it, to no avail. My feet bore two microscopic bite marks, but there was no swelling. To make matters worse, the pain subsided by the time Diana changed the sheets. And still no centipede!

In retrospect, it could have been a dream. (Only a 10% possibility. Of course, my insistence to Diana that I had been bitten might be skewing my probabilities.) How could a dream give such intense pain, enough to shock me conscious?

Clearly God was telling me something. First, I thought He was telling me that I was watching too much TV. I got caught up in the

Olympics and was watching every night. However, earlier in the year I had answered God's call to become a pastor and had started my studies, but was slacking off. So I returned to my regular routine.

Then, on **Wednesday, August 27**, I had another dream: "Centipede crawling on me—arm? I woke up to shake it off. This was two days after the bite on my left Achilles heel." (figure 4, page 43)

On **Friday, August 29**, after I had shared my centipede stories, Jason shared that he had a dream on **Saturday, August 23** (a week prior). In his dream, the government was wondering why A-1 was doing so well on the big government project. He had seen **Nick Vujicic**, the evangelist without limbs, and realized that God was blessing us for others (like Nick). A-1 had nothing to hide; we weren't doing anything illegal or unethical. But God is sovereign and can use fear to prompt necessary action.

After Jason shared his dream, I recognized that the two centipede situations were not about my studies but about God getting me back on my mission. God had given A-1 a healthy backlog of work that would last for years. He did so during the worst global economic recession. I was still following our "Joseph Plan," but God made it obvious that I was choking the flow of funds to His ministries. I loosened my grip and increased giving.

God was also redirecting the focus of my mission: Becoming a pastor wasn't the only thing God desired. He also wanted to give birth to Cedar Assembly of God. We formally incorporated the church in late 2010. And then God moved us to **All Peoples Mission Church** on Waipa Lane.

When I first started preaching the English services at Hawaii Cedar Church, I would preach then run away. Actually, Diana and I attended the early service at First Assembly of God, then left to preach the English service at 11 a.m. Then I'd hurry off to squeeze in a lunch date with my bride. When we moved into our own church building, our people started saying, "This is our home church!" So we didn't run away, we served them lunch and ate with them. Now they say, "This is my family!" God had to send a Ninja centipede to activate His plan and get me moving in the right direction.

GOD'S DREAM: "THIS IS YOUR HELPER!"

Jesus said: *"You did not choose me, but I chose you and **appointed you** to go and bear fruit — fruit that will last"* (Jn. 15:16). This isn't limited to God drawing us to Jesus, it also includes Him choosing His team. God knows which people to bring together for the mission with the necessary gifts, resources, talents, culture, and history. They say God works in mysterious ways but I say He works in hilarious ways. Here's a story of how He brought a pastor out of a Vegas addict.

Darrick and Melissa "Missy" Nakata were born and raised in Honolulu. They knew each other from "small kid time" but didn't connect until after high school. Each went through God's "Seminary of Suffering" until they were ready for His call.

In 2006, both of them were stuck in reverse and headed for a fiery crash-and-burn in Sin City. Darrick was at the end of his rope. He went to his mother-in-law's room to borrow money for a "fix." She was sleeping. Darrick curled up on the floor next to her bed and cried out to God. A few days later, he was walking to a bus stop to get to work. A Las Vegas cop stopped him and asked for identification.

As the officer ran a check, Darrick was cleared and she almost let him go. But she went back to her squad car and hurried back: He had a bench warrant for a parole violation in Hawaii. She arrested him on the spot. The police also went to his residence and arrested Missy. They were thrown in jail until they were extradited to Hawaii. One of the best places for a drug addict is in jail; they both detoxed. By the time they arrived in Hawaii, they were almost clean.

They spent another 30 days in jail in Hawaii. Total time in jail: 75 days. The first thing they did was catch the bus to Waikiki and they began to see God's Hand. What makes Hawaii a special place is Ohana (family). First, they didn't have bus fare, but the bus driver let them hop on. Then they did what the homeless do in Waikiki: They headed to the beach and saw God's Hand provide a large air mattress for their bed. Eventually God led them to Kapiolani Park. **Pastor Tuia and Dottie Fale** had started a homeless outreach there and brought food.

One Friday night, Pastor Tuia didn't have a chance to pick-up sandwiches. After the meeting Darrick was still hungry; so he prayed out loud, **"Lord, if You are real, give me a sign: Bring food!"** A wedding couple showed up with pans of food from their reception. Darrick and Missy received the Lord. (God knows the way to a man's heart is through his stomach!)

The couple started helping Pastor Tuia. But just as things started looking up, the cops came to clean out the park. Darrick didn't want a ticket as that would be a parole violation. He heard that **Next Step Shelter** was open so he and Missy applied and got a cubicle. (figure 5, page 44)

Soon after, Darrick and Missy heard about a church that gave free gifts but they held back not wanting to go just for the gifts. But God drew them and eventually they came to Hawaii Cedar Church. They realized gifts from God were not bad after all, as long as their hearts were right.

Sometimes you can measure people's growth by how far they sit from the pulpit. The first time I noticed them, they were sitting way in the back. Then they moved a little closer, and again closer, until they were right up in the third row. In August 2009, they approached me to ask if I would perform their wedding. After being together 20 years, they were finally married on September 6, 2009. Hallelujah! They came to church every day the doors were open and helped in many ways.

In time, **Pastor Russell Uehara** got permission to go into **Next Step** to host a Bible study. Darrick accompanied Russell. On Monday, July 12, 2010 Russell had Darrick run the Bible study and Russell later sent an email telling me that Darrick had done a great job. On Tuesday night, July 13, 2010, God sent me a dream: "Darrick leading Bible Study." I saw him on a picnic table at Next Step under a light with a few others. *Was God sending me the dream so Cedar could take the next step to commit to Darrick and Missy?* Next, I had to ask Darrick and Missy if they wanted to be a part of the ministry.

At this point Darrick and Missy were about to end their two-year stay at Next Step. They were considering transitional housing in Waianae. We met and they committed to being "all in." They were planning to minister even if they moved. That weekend, I went to Craigslist to shop for apartments. On Wednesday, July 21, we drove around and found a perfect location on Rose Street, not far from church. By Saturday, July 24 (Missy's birthday), the owner committed to rent to them. God needed just 12 days to help Darrick and Missy secure a home and make a long-term commitment to ministry. Twelve days! That's double the time He needed to create the universe!

Darrick is now **Pastor Darrick** and is walking through the process to become a certified pastor. God chose Darrick and Missy and He has a good plan for them. *"Brothers, choose seven men from among you who are known to be full of the Spirit and wisdom"* (Acts 6:3). God's criteria was to be full of Spirit and wisdom. For Pastor Darrick and Missy's selection criteria, God gave us these:

1. Hungry for the Word and for a deeper relationship with Jesus.

2. Active participation in serving.

3. A heart for the homeless and the poor.

4. They were "all in."

As I look back, it's clear God sent a dream guiding me to my assistant pastor. God's timing was perfect. Darrick is my assistant pastor, my operational pastor, my "go-to" pastor, my "do-all" pastor! And Missy has taken on operational and leadership roles. God chose them, provided a new life, a new home, and a new family. (figure 6, page 44)

GOD SENDS FIRST RESPONDERS

Earl Sumner was doing some heavy drinking in Chinatown one night when a huge guy approached with his right hand behind his back. The guy, tattoos all over his left arm, asked, "If you were to die tonight, do you know where you'd go?" Earl and his drinking buddy thought, *Oh, no! We're gonna die tonite!* The guy pulled out a Bible and witnessed to them. They both got saved and were invited to come up to a place in Manoa for fellowship and food. Earl didn't know what fellowship was, but he knew food.

That group was **Youth With a Mission** (YWAM) and the first to plant a YWAM base in Hawaii. When I asked Earl what he liked about them, he said he liked the family unity. One night he went up to the YWAM house to join them in witnessing downtown. One of the girls felt the Lord told her they should go up to the Pali lookout and worship Him. Earl was bummed so while the team went to the lookout, he and a friend went witnessing instead. (That was his passion. Earl later became a pastor!)

That night, a young girl came running to the YWAM team crying hysterically that her boyfriend had fallen and begging for help. The leader ran to an emergency phone box (no cell phones at that time) and called 911. The operator took the information and responded that police and ambulance would pick up the body the next day. The leader insisted, telling him that God would not have sent them to the lookout if the guy who fell was going to die. They were sent to save him!

Because of his insistence, an emergency team arrived and the rescue is history: That fallen young man became Hawaii evangelist Danny Yamashiro. (To see his astonishing life story, check out Danny's website, http://dannyyamashiro.org/, and click "Against All Odds.") Surely God's Hand caught him that night! God-dreams save lives!

SOMETIMES YOU HAVE TO LEAVE FAMILY TO GROW THE FAMILY

God introduced us to Tom and Cindy Bauer in 1999 and we've been intimately and eternally woven together ever since: Our families, ministries, even our business as we supported them and their team prayed for our business. I'd see Tom and Cindy at least once or twice a week. Like the Acts church, our families shared meals, Tom and I had sushi often, and we enjoyed double dates with our wives.

Ministry is tough. When God called us to Hawaii Cedar Church and later Cedar AOG, Tom volunteered to help pastor the church. (Can you imagine Tom as my assistant? God has a neat sense of humor!) Although we'd stopped Daven's Bible study with STN in late 2003, I was still teaching a weekly Bible study with them. I was also on their Board of Directors.

By mid-2010, the churches and ministries God had me in were taking a lot of time. Plus, I was still working with A-1 A-Lectrician. I started praying what the Lord would have me to do, and I felt a tugging on my heart that He wanted me to leave STN. *Whoa! That's my spiritual family!*

On Tuesday, **September 14, 2010**, for the first time in my life I laid a double fleece before the Lord. "If it is okay to leave STN, Lord, show me a dream with a broken surfboard. Second, if it's okay to leave our 'Men for Christ' Bible study, show me an empty plate." That very night, I had a double dream:

1ˢᵗ Part —"STN dinner—plates empty" — I'm at a Surfing the Nations dinner and my plate is empty. The fleece I asked for was an empty plate; God showed it to me and gave His okay.

2ⁿᵈ Part —"Buying van—2-seater, $20 G's (Grand), 6-seater – $40G's.

"Daven and Lisa—use for beach, but nothing in van. Van looks cheapy—windows look riveted together. We test driving. It stands up to driving. We not carrying any surfboards or boogie boards, but intent was for beach with kids. New direction in Life?"

In this I dream, I was looking to purchase a van. The van shows life direction/mission. We intended to use it for the beach with Daven and Lisa (both did STN missions to Bali). But it was empty: no surfboards in a van meant for surfing. It as clear what God was saying: It's time to leave STN.

The next day, Thursday, **September 16**, STN had a board meeting and I broke the news:

To: Board of Directors, Surfing the Nations & Surfers Church
Subject: Resignation of Jimmy Yamada

Due to a tremendous increase in time required for ministries that I am now involved in (many struggling and others just starting), I regret to inform you that effective Thurs., 9/16/10, after the STN Board Meeting, I will be resigning from the STN Board and Surfers Church. I will also do my last scheduled STN Bible study on Thurs., Oct 14.

It has been an honor and a privilege being with your awesome organization and I am saddened that we have come to this juncture. However, God is going to continue to bless you. He wants me to focus. We've made a financial commitment to STN/Surfers Church and intend to fulfill that commitment.

We continue to pray for STN and you all will continue to hold a very special place in our hearts.

AGAPE,

Jimmy & Diana Yamada (& Family)

At the Board Meeting, I took out the letter and started reading, but before I could start the second paragraph, I began to weep uncontrollably. I had to hand the letter to **Charis Bauer** and asked her to continue reading. We were all weeping, but it was a good cry: *"Paul answered, 'Why are you weeping and breaking my heart?'"* (Acts 21:13). As God guides our steps in ministry, He brings both good times and sad. There's still joy as we all know we will remain connected by His Spirit in our different ministries.

Tom and I still get to eat sushi, but not as often. We still go on double dates, but not as often. It's the price of serving the Lord.

GOD TURNS OVER CONTROL SO HE CAN BE IN CONTROL

My biggest problem is actually a very small one; I want to be in control. If it wasn't for that, I'd be perfect! (Of course, I'm joking! My humor needs as much help as my humility.) God doesn't seem to be very helpful as He gave me gifts and talents for His plan, then has me "come to my senses." So it's all God's fault. *Hah!* Seriously, though, many struggle and are *not joking* about blaming God for their choices.

Much of my Christian journey has been spent on the issue of control. Author **C.S. Lewis** wrote that our great sin is pride. **Who is in control of my life?** My thoughts? My wife? (I truly thought that was my job.) Who's in control of my family? My business, A-1? My work? My church? These are only the *tip* of the control iceberg: **Who is in control?**

God has been so smooth that I didn't catch on until too late that He was tricking me to actually ***want* Him to be in control!** Miraculous! (LOL) And the greatest coup? God orchestrated the hand over of our family business. For me to be more like Jesus, God needed to put control into Jason's hands.

God did that by aligning everything in my life, Jason's life, and our world to bring His plan to pass. First, He gave Jason the skill-set he would need to run the business: In school and college, and then on-the-job training in his first years at A-1. And just as God did with Olympian **Eric Liddell** ("Chariots of Fire"), He made Jason fast: Fast to catch on, fast in sports; and even fast to live life in the fast lane. He went out for football his freshman year and came back the first day only to say: "Dad, I'm not playing football. There's a big 6'2" guy who is 220 pounds. (Jason was 5'6".) And he's fast!" So Jason stuck to wrestling and judo. He knew where he wanted to be.

Jason went to University of Hawaii and took five and a half years to graduate. He wasn't in a rush. He could surf, party (his backslidden years) and cruise. He had his fast cars, fast body boards and was living a fast life. God touched his life one season and brought him back to Jesus.

When Jason graduated, I sat down with him to discuss what he wanted to do with his life. I honestly wanted him to do what God wanted. (God was healing my "control-itis" disease.) I said, "Jason you can go anywhere to work and make $30,000-$35,000/year. Or you can be an electrician and earn $55,000/year." Jason was smart, he became an electrician.

GOD AUTHORS A-1'S NEXT CHAPTER

Electricians are skilled workers who build complex systems where people work, live, shop, and play. Electrical systems are a crucial part of a building, comparable to blood vessels in your body. It connects every part of your body and your body (or building) doesn't work without it. It's an vital job.

By his first year as a full-time electrician, Jason had already worked 10 summers out in the field. I remember one day he came home after "roughing in the deck" (laying conduits in the concrete deck). It was at One Waterfront Towers, a twin 40-story condominium. He said, "Dad, I smoked everyone!" (he was the first to finish the rough). As he tried to excel, Jason set a pace to race against everyone. He didn't realize that no one else was racing.

In fact, the other electricians encouraged him to keep it up, so he kept racing. Hard work gets you more work; but God's Hand was in that too. (Thank you to all the A-1 leaders who helped train and develop Jason. I'm glad, as I know you are, that you did a good job because now he's your boss.)

As a lead-off mechanic, Jason eventually became foreman on the Navy Commissary Project. Eventually Jason was promoted to project engineer, then project manager. And because he was a fast learner, he was promoted to Vice President of Operations at 28 years of age. And soon Jason achieved the greatest promotion in our company at the age of 32 (2009): President and Chief Operating Officer.

Another important milestone was when I turned over all estimating to him later that same year. Jason felt it was too early as he was overseeing a large project that was nine months from completion. All the critical electrical systems were just coming on line. It was a mountainous task and at the same time a splendid opportunity for Jason to grow.

Add to that the economic fallout from the subprime debacle was a year old (2009) and things looked dark. At that time, I was ready to go *"all in"* and become a pastor and form a church. God had transplanted my passion from needing construction to people-in-need.

Both Diana and I had clearly heard from God: Jason was God's man to take over. However, there was a small issue of control: My instruction to Jason was to follow Peter Drucker's business principles.

If he was going to deviate, he must "check in" with me. The problem with this logic is that the next generation may follow the same principles but they have their own paradigm. We "old guys" tend to see things through "old guy" paradigm. The young never know when they deviate until the "old guys" complain and tell them they're doing it wrong. To correct my "control-itis," God sent me dreams...

GOD'S DREAM: "TIME TO MOVE ON"

The first dream involved me playing poker with a contractor. He was doing something not kosher. I took that as a sign that we shouldn't do business with him. So I told Jason my dream but I also told him to hear from God and make the final decision. Jason decided to pursue the work and things went smoothly. That made me think, *Hmm*....

Second communication from God involved two dreams: **January 6, 2011**: First, I'm part of an Engineering Architectural team building something. I leave the group and get lost trying to find the road. Second, I'm traveling alone. I didn't understand this until I put it together with the next dream...

January 11, 2011: "I'm in a large building. Had an outage (loss of power). I need to notify building owner of potential trouble. Fix = Main HECO (Hawaiian Electric Co.). The bus duct leading into building/project was unprotected and not encased w/concrete. If blowup and someone die, big liability. I meet with owner and he wants me to draw up on newspaper."

A number of things were wrong with this dream: HECO would not own and install a bus duct system like this. Also, an electrical bus duct system (carrying main incoming electricity) would not be installed in concrete encasement. To warn the building owner of the danger would have been off base.

At this time, A-1 was working on a project where Jason was thinking about filing a mechanics lien (a lawsuit laying claim to ownership). He asked me about it and I advised that I thought it might be a good idea, but I left it to him. Jason decided against it. **Revelation**: I realized the lien was a tool in God's Hand to reveal a bigger issue: Complete control of A-1. God had been telling me many things in my dreams and He tied them all together with the lien issue. Here was the ultimate revelation:

1. I played poker with an old paradigm. It was not relevant to Jason.
2. I got lost walking with the Engineering Architectural team and end up alone. Meaning: I am not up with the current state of construction. I was "state of the art"…about 30 years ago. *Duh!*
3. In the outage dream, God showed I'm not up on electrical code either. My book is no longer the National Electrical Codebook but the Bible. It's better for Jason to ask Jesus, not "Junior" (my nickname).
4. The lien confirmed that Jason needed to stop looking to me and look entirely to God.

The following week, I met with Jason to share what God was telling me. I looked my son in the eye and told him: "**I believe that God wants me to give you full control of the business and you don't have to check with me on anything. You need to hear from God.**"

Jason is fast, and the first thing he asked me was, "Dad, can I fire you?" "*YES!*" I fired right back. He smiled and returned to his work. Complete responsibility and authority had just been transferred in a five-minute meeting. It doesn't take long when all parties are ultimately controlled by God.

PS: Jason and I still talk business.

5

FAMILY DREAMS

DIANA'S DREAMS

My wife was born Diana Enokawa, full of God's grace, favor and blessing. Her family was poor in finances but rich in the things money cannot buy. That richness came as a result of God's grace and their decision to live righteously, the best they could. The Enokawa kids were no angels but they stuck together and God kept them strong. Their tight bond kept them on the right path.

Diana always had God's favor and He connected her to a group of girlfriends who were well-off. Their families worked good jobs and owned small businesses. None were millionaires but they were better off than 90% of their schoolmates at Central Intermediate. Most of their peers lived in poverty; many from public housing and only a few were middle class. It was a rough-and-tough school.

Diana's early childhood friends were the predecessors of the Les Charmaines, a YMCA club. They had the beauty, brains, and the boys. Lady Gaga had nothing over the Les Charmaines. But having a lot usually leads to wanting more. (figure 7, page 45)

One day the school principal called in the whole club. (Those were the good old days when teachers and administrators had authority over students.) They had been cutting school and going downtown, having fun, and even "borrowing" things from stores. The girls were in big trouble, all except for Diana. God had watched over her and kept her from "borrowing."

Diana's older sister, Doris had polio at an early age. Yet it never stopped her from growing, walking, and becoming a budding entrepreneur. She was quite a bit older than the rest of the Enokawa kids and became a second mother. She passed on that "can do" attitude to her siblings.

Doris bought knickknacks to make trinkets which she sold for a nickel (or whatever she could get). She got her supplies at the Kress Store downtown on Fort Street Mall. It was the hot place to get everything you needed. Diana accompanied her and was enamored by it all.

Diana had a dream where she was hiding downstairs in Kress: "I was waiting for the store to close. Once everyone was gone, I came out of hiding with the intent of taking all that my heart was set on: candy, new clothes and, best of all, trinkets and toys. Suddenly a statue-like figure came floating down the stairs, gliding over the floors. It resembled the statue of Jesus (figure 8, page 45) in Brazil on the top of the mountain. Frantically, I tried to get away, crawling along the floor, but He kept coming. I felt like He knew what I had planned. I tried to look at His face, but the light was too bright."

Diana is sure that God came to keep her on the straight and narrow. Even when her friends were in mischief, she was protected. She looks back with fondness knowing God gave her a terrifying dream to protect her.

GOD INCUBATES DIANA

One of Diana's recurring dreams as a child was at Kauluwela Elementary: (figure 9, page 46) "I was in a corner of the big open field, standing on a stone wall. The whole field was enclosed; either by buildings, walls, or a chain link fence. Directly in front of me was water and there were sharks in the water. Beyond the water was green grass. I was trapped with fear."

Interpretation: God was incubating Diana.

1. Field enclosed – God was protecting her like the Hebrews in Egypt.
2. Standing on a stone wall – represents Jesus. Although Diana was not saved, she had God. God sent her the Kress Store dream. Also, her Mom had her children go to **Salvation Army Church**. And God used her older brother Marvin to protect her. The sharks wouldn't even think about coming after Diana.
3. Sharks in the water — Predators after Diana and surrounding her in the world.
4. Green grass beyond — A better life later. God was incubating Diana. All of her friends went to McKinley or Farrington High Schools. God brought her to the green grass of Roosevelt. Thank God! ☺

DIANA'S SPIRITUAL TEAM

Diana leads a team of angels to a place close to her heart, Leahi Hospital. It's where God took Pop, Diana's father. It was a peaceful homegoing for Pop, but difficult for Diana because she grew closer to him during his last 5 years than in her previous 50. But God used Diana's affinity for the hospital to draw her back. She started volunteering in 2004 as a "Lone Rangeress." God soon brought a small army.

In the beginning, Diana was the youngest; the other, older women were blessed to serve again as they thought their useful days were behind them. They had a hard time getting around as none drove. Now Diana drove and it was a treat to go out, especially at night! They could "boogie" again.

They began their outreach with the practical gospel: songs, dances, jokes, comedy routines, neck massages. Then Diana brought food: *natto* (Japanese fermented soybeans) for the older Japanese ladies, *maki sushi*, *manju* and tasty snacks. But the staff worried about their patients' health, so they stopped the flow of food, except for the *natto*.

One great bonus was the "afterglow": Going out to eat afterwards. Favorites included Wailana Coffee Shop, or Chinese, Japanese, American and Thai restaurants. If someone had a birthday, they had a celebration. This allowed them to develop into God's ultimate blessing, a family.

One of the women, Mrs. Nishie, often shared her blessings. She was an 80-year-old woman when she started with Diana, and had worked diligently all her life. From "small kid time," Mrs. Nishie had carried a 100-pound bag of rice. Her father taught her never to waste even a single grain. She got saved at First Assembly of God at an early age, married, raised a family, and bought a house. Her Dad would have been proud: She could afford to waste rice but she never did. As part of the "Greatest Generation," she held strong to her values. Diana is a natural for food, fun, and fellowship and God used these talents to restore the other women's dreams to serve Him to the fullness of their lives.

DAVEN'S DREAM: "YOU'RE IN THE RIGHT PLACE"

The absolute worst thing that can ever happen to grandparents is to have a grandchild kidnapped. This happened to us in July 2013: Our son and his wife Charity (figure 10, page 46) kidnapped their daughter Madison (Madi) and moved to California. We recognized it was part of God's plan; they were both pastors and missionaries with Every Nation. (But it was still kidnapping.)

We released Daven early on to find God's call for his life. After high school, we let him find a church and ministry that he liked. Parents tend to interfere, but it's important to let your grown children find their own way. As they do, God will guide and work out good for their lives, and they'll see it! The Bible teaches that God will connect them to their mission (Jer. 29:11, Isa. 46:10-11).

And now as pastors fulfilling God's call to California, they had to hear from Him in three top areas: church, ministry and work. They started by locating Every Nation churches, however, the two closest ones were almost an hour away. But before the move, Daven had a dream (figure 11, page 47) and he sketched it out. One day they visited a church right in their hometown, Valley Bible Church. As Daven drove up, he had *deja vu*, and took a picture of what he saw: It was the same driveway he'd seen in his dream. (figure 12, page 47) God was confirming their new home church.

I had written a poem and sang it at their goodbye party (to Matt Redmond's, "10,000 Reasons"):
"And on that day with our family leaving
Our hearts are sad but our God is glad
So we know there will be no grieving
10,000 souls will see the light of day
Bless the Lord oh my soul...."

Nothing can be greater than to see God's Hand in our children as He confirms His dream for their lives.

BREAD COMES TO LIFE

Next on the agenda was to find a home — a hub for church, ministry and work. They started looking and I hit my computer. My criteria: No major fault lines or flood zones, and stay high above sea level to protect against tsunamis. After all, God did say that in the Last Days, there will be earthquakes and resulting tidal waves. The fault lines and tsunamis were easy. The flooding zones were more difficult. So I downloaded FEMA (Federal Emergency Management Agency) flood maps for the city of Vallejo. Daven used those maps and weaned out unacceptable neighborhoods. We also factored in schools and crime.

Daven and Charity looked at dozens of houses and drove around to get a feel for the area they may eventually call home. Trying to find a home was like finding the proverbial needle in a haystack. One day while driving through one of their target neighborhoods they saw an "Open House" sign. It wasn't on their list so their realtor called the agent. It was the first house they really liked; but it was already sold.

I asked Daven for the address so we could find similar models. The area was about six years old and there were no models, but we locked in on square footage and used that as our model number: "2767 SF." We kept searching. One night, I got an e-mail, "This could be the one!" They arranged to see the house the next day. *It was the same house!*

What struck Daven was a month earlier he had a dream about bread. God connected it to their house but he had no idea what the connection was. Every house he entered he looked for the sign: "God, show me the bread!" When they went through the kitchen of this house, Daven saw a glass door for the pantry. A closer look revealed a beautiful etching of bread. (figure 13, page 48)

They proceeded upstairs and the master bedroom blew their minds: It was huge. They looked out and saw a beautiful view of the ninth hole of a golf course. God had showed them the house where they were to plant their future lives: the house where they would bring up Madi, and where future ministry opportunities would be launched. God had designed and reserved this house specifically for them.

A KANGAROO HAT?

You can move God by prayer or be moved by God when you pray. You can fall in love with the beauty that God created or you can love God because of His beauty. I choose all of the above!

The night I almost died, I saw Diana walk to me carrying Jason in her arms and Daven in her belly; she was five months pregnant. God loved Jason and Daven and saved me from hell. Life would have ended very differently for our family if God had not sent an angel to protect me that fateful night.

Daven was born special. I can only remember having to give him 10 super-chais (spankings). God gave him favor because when he saw his older brother, Jason, get a few super-super-chais, God drew out the angel in him.

God called him into ministry early and blessed him with his bride, Charity, and now my beautiful granddaughter, **Madison Hope Yamada**. Daven first connected with STN, then Every Nations Ministries in his walk to becoming a pastor. He started serving with **Pastor Daven Hee** at Innovative Concepts Church; they held services at Dave and Busters. (Truly innovative, wouldn't you say?) Thank you **Pastor Daven Hee** and his wife **Barbie** for mentoring Daven and Charity.

One day a friend, Ron, asked Daven to pray for another friend ("Guy") who was in the hospital. Pastor Daven, my son Daven and Charity went with Ron to Queen's Hospital to visit Guy. They spent time with him and Pastor Daven explained the Gospel. Charity had the honor of praying with him to receive the Lord. Guy had a tumor in his neck the size of a large apple; he died the following week.

A week later, Daven had a dream: He saw Guy completely healthy and, oddly enough, wearing a Kangol golfer's hat. The next time Dave saw Ron he told him about his dream and mentioned the hat. Ron was overwhelmed. He said that Guy had always worn a Kangol hat. Daven never knew that. God showed them that Guy was in heaven. It was a great encouragement for their faith!

CHARITY'S DREAM: AN ATTACK

Charity grew up in a Catholic home in Hercules, California. Her parents bought the home in the mid-70s after they married and had saved the down payment. Charity's mom, **Femme**, was a secretary for an insurance brokerage firm. Her dad, **Napoleon**, worked for the Federal Reserve; he counted money all day. In 1999, Charity moved to Hawaii to attend Hawaii Pacific University (HPU) and got connected to a Christian group on campus. She eventually found the Lord, got saved (2000) and ended up leading the club with two friends. They became Every Nations campus ministers and actively ministered to the students. Their program encouraged them to live life together and so all three moved into a ministry house in lower Aiea, right below where Daven lived.

One night, God sent a dream. An e-mail from Charity explains: "I prayed the salvation prayer and invited Christ into my heart and life in the Fall of 2000. About 1 year later, I moved into a student house that was run by my local church. One night, I experienced something for the first time:

"I had a dream in the middle of the night and from what I remember, there was this dark figure, either coming at me and/or trying to reach for me. It almost looked like a monk with a black-hooded robe but the face I couldn't make out. My natural instinct was to call out to my roommate for help, but every time I tried to yell for her nothing would come out of my mouth. It was as if someone was stopping me from speaking. It was also hard to move, as if someone was holding me down. It was such a helpless and scary feeling, but thank God that I eventually woke up and whatever hold on me was released."

In interpreting dreams, since it is not always clear, it's best to list possibilities. Here is the ever-important context: After coming to Jesus, Charity was an evangelist preacher. In fact, God used that to bring Daven and Charity together. Daven had known Charity for years through Every Nations, but only as a fellow soldier in the Lord's Army. Daven finally "noticed" Charity in May 2006 as she was telling a story about ministry at HPU. As she shared one particular woman's story, she began to weep. God used that to awaken love in Daven and, two months later, he revealed that he had feelings for her. She shared that she also had feelings for him. The rest is His-story.

A few interpretations for Charity:

Option 1: God revealed that Satan will continually try to disrupt your ministry, so beware!

Option 2: God revealed that Satan will try to stop you from moving freely for Jesus' sake; beware!

Option 3: God wants you to know He'll always deliver you from Satan's attacks, so never be afraid!

These are all very similar in nature and God could have been warning her about all three, perhaps more. I do not believe Satan came to visit her or sent the dream; God sent it to encourage and warn her.

GOD HAS A JOB SET ASIDE

Charity spent the last half of 2014 looking for a job. She didn't want to drive too far, and she was seeking a position in Human Resources. She sent applications to over 25 companies, only a couple responded. The problem? Vallejo declared bankruptcy back in 2008 and was the largest city in California to do so at that time. It had an unemployment rate of 15% in 2010, which had fallen to 8% when Charity was job-hunting. Daven and Charity knew the obstacles were huge, but they also knew their God.

Here's an e-mail from Daven on **December 3, 2014**: "Charity took a test week and a half ago for an HR position in Vacaville. Good location, part-time hours, good hourly. She was excited since it was her first bite out of all jobs she applied for. When she went, there were 100+ applicants testing for the job! She felt she did pretty well on the test but was doubtful because there were so many people.

"While Charity was waiting on the results last week, she had a dream she didn't get the job and was actually invited to take another exam for an old job she applied for. In the dream she thought it was West America Bank. When she told me, I thought it meant she might not get the Vacaville job but that maybe she would get another job from a place she applied before. [Keep that in mind.]

"She found out on Monday that she was not selected to move on in the testing for the HR position in Vacaville. She was pretty bummed as it was the first invite she got, and also since it's been about 5 months that she has been applying.

"However, just yesterday she got an e-mail from Erlinda (Ryan's cousin's wife) about another HR Generalist job opening in Vallejo at Touro University. She was doubtful because the qualification and experience were well beyond what Charity has and normally companies want someone already qualified. She explained that to Erlinda but said she was interested if they were open to training her. Erlinda passed the message on to her friend at Touro.

"Just today, they said they were still interested and asked to see her resume. This afternoon the HR Director called her and SHE HAS AN INTERVIEW TOMORROW MORNING AT 10am!! If the interview goes well, she will start on Monday! They interviewed 3 people already but none of them had the right skill set they were looking for.

"They also said they were open to training Charity on the software she didn't know. The main program she needs to know is Microsoft Excel, which Charity knows well since all our church rosters, forms, and documents were done using Excel! The job is about 10 minutes away and its right here in Vallejo. Its a temp job right now as someone is going on Maternity leave, December through Mid April.

"It lines right up with the dream because Charity applied for another job at Touro University back when we moved here but it didn't work out. That opening was also a reference from Erlinda.

"Pray the interview goes well tomorrow!"

The interview went well and Charity was hired; she started the following Monday. God didn't say she would get the job, only that she was **"invited to take another exam for an old job she applied for."** It's a walk of faith. God gives us just enough; we have to walk it out step by step.

LISA'S DREAM: "SOMEONE'S CHASING ME!"

As a Dad, I always felt that my baby girl Lisa could do anything she ever wanted to do. God was working for her good and used Diana to develop her gifts and talent. Mom always read to Lisa Girl, ever since she was just two years old. Her Aunty Elaine and Aunty Doris wrote stories on toilet paper scrolls and Diana would read them to her. She also read her children's books and all sorts of stories. Lisa would ask at bedtime, "Mom, can you read to me?" Diana would reply, "Lisa, when are you going to sleep by yourself?" Lisa would answer, "When I'm four." The answer, inevitably, was always the *next* year. By that time, Diana had usually been up for 14 hours of "full-speed ahead" and so she'd always drop into a deep sleep after about 15 minutes. When Lisa was nearing her teen years, she said, "Mom, can you sleep in your own room?" That was the end of reading time; but it was also the start of Lisa's journalism career.

Lisa graduated from Pepperdine University with a degree in journalism and a 3.9 GPA. She never got anything less than an A-. (Cool way to brag about your kids, just write a book!) God used Diana to stimulate Lisa's love of reading, writing, and communication, and she excelled at it.

Upon graduation in 2008, Lisa returned home to a dismal job market in the midst of a recession. She ended up working for a short time at A-1 A-Lectrician. Still wanting to put her degree to use and tell stories that she knew were missing in the marketplace, she started an arts-and-culture magazine called *Flux Hawaii*. In 2012 she partnered with **Jason Cutinella** in his content-producing company, **Nella Media Group**. The dream? To form a media empire and they're well on their way. Their magazines include *Kikaha*, an inflight magazine for **Island Air**, and *+Table*, a hotel coffee table book with a readership of more than 3.5 million domestic and international travelers in the State of Hawaii. They'll soon take their brand national, making marketing trips to Los Angeles and New York City, the center of budding moguls.

Lisa had a repeating dream when she was very young: She was in a grocery store being chased by clowns. (Like the movie, "Killer Klowns from Outer Space.") Years later, she can still see herself hiding in the store's control room, watching the clowns on the security cameras, the grainy black-and-white, eerie smile of the clowns clear as day. Her dad, who thinks he can interpret dreams, thinks God is showing her that the world is chasing after her, and it seems so. As an executive editorial and creative director, Lisa is a big whip. People want to write for her. Others want their stories to be covered. Advertisers want products publicized. And models want to be the next "face" in Hawaii's fashion and arts world. They all want Lisa's nod. God knows the future and lets us know that.

GOD ANNOUNCES "YOUR BUSINESS WILL EXPAND!"

Dae Son was born in Korea and came to Hawaii when he was four years old. In Hawaii, there are three groups of Koreans: First generation (born in Korea, arrived as adults), second generation (people born here) and the "1.5 generation" (born in Korea and grew up here). The 1.5 generation are typically between 6-10 years old upon arrival and have one foot in Korea and one in America. Dae is a "1.5er." Lisa and Dae met in 2011. Dae is very quiet and has joined us at family dinners.

One day, while Lisa was off changing the world in New York, Dae showed up on my doorstep and told me he wanted to surprise Lisa with a visit. He asked me for her hand. After I joyfully welcomed him into the family, he showed me the engagement ring. "I hope that's fake!" I gasped. But Dae is part of what made America a great nation, he's a small businessman and a skilled craftsman. He makes custom, hand-crafted hardwood furniture. (figure 14, page 48)

Dae started his business in 2013. It's a small 200-square-foot space on the second floor of a warehouse. A Good Samaritan businessman wanted to give young budding businesses a start and knew they needed space. It was perfect for Dae — the rent was right and he could work on the furniture he loved to build. One problem: It was on the second floor so getting the big pieces of wood up to his space was tough! But Dae is Korean-strong and a hard worker.

Early in 2014, Dae had a dream of his landlord asking if he'd like to move into a bigger space downstairs. Dae took it and saw himself working in a 20-by-20-foot space. The dream was God announcing to Dae: "Your business will expand."

One week later, to Dae's surprise, his landlord approached him and offered the very workspace he had seen in his dream. The landlord told Dae he had "first choice" and encouraged him to take it. However, Dae's business couldn't afford the increased rent and he told the landlord so. But since the space wouldn't be available for a few months, the landlord said he could wait. A few months later, Dae landed a contract to build three large tables for Turtle Bay Resort. He had the means and the reason for increased space. He took the space. But the young furniture-maker worried the space was still a little too large. So the landlord installed a partition so Dae could have just the right space. Six months later, Dae's business continued to grow and the new downstairs space is now too small.

God's dream through Dae lets us know that He cares about every detail and is working it all out.

JASON'S DREAM: "GIVE US A SIGN"

One of the great joys of parenting is to train your kids to do things they love on their own. Our kids did judo, soccer, ballet, swimming, basketball, and volleyball. Some for a season, some for years. Further, family activities included surfing, body boarding, shoreline fishing, deep-sea fishing, diving, torching, camping and shopping. As Dad, my focus of all of this activity was the training, development and discipline of my children. After we found Jesus, we also wanted them to find their calling and mission.

Jason found his mission in the family business and became president. He willingly took on its challenges knowing God is with Him. Jason recognizes he's responsible to God for all that happens in the business.

One day A-1 was working on a large project. To give context, once a developer decides to build a project, he selects a general contractor who works with subcontractors during the job's design phase. So both the developer and the general contractor must select a list of subcontractors. A-1 was one of two electrical subs in consideration. Jason called me for advice and I shared what I normally did in difficult situations: Lay a fleece before the Lord and ask for a dream. A-1 had been working on this project for nearly six months and Jason wanted to secure it.

Jason laid a double fleece: "Lord if you don't think we should be involved in the project, give me a dream to scare me away." (Jason believes the Lord always answers: yes, no, or wait.) If the Lord did not send him a dream to scare him, that would be confirmation that he should pursue it. The Lord did not send a dream. In our thinking, since the Lord always answers, lack of a dream meant "go for it."

Jason then laid a second fleece as he prepared to negotiate the job: He asked the Lord to let the general contractor make a request that would scare him away. That would be a sign **not** to pursue it. A few days later, the general contractor called and made reasonable requests—a green light for securing the project. The Lord answered twice: First, in the absence of a dream, and then in positive negotiations.

DONNA'S DREAM: "DON'T LET GO!"

Donna Kyong Pak came from Korea with her father and two sisters in the early 80s. She was the oldest and since her mother didn't come with them to America, Donna was like a mother to her sisters. Their father remarried and she had a stepbrother. Their family is close, especially as their father passed away in the late 1990s. (figure 15, page 49)

Jason dated Donna for a few years. One day I asked if he loved her and could spend the rest of his life with her. He answered, "Yeah." "Then what are you waiting for?" I asked. A few months later I got a call during family dinner. Jason and Donna had gone to Vegas and were getting married the next day. "Wait," I said, "talk to your Mom," and handed the phone to Diana. Diana was bummed but not for long; she's strong. When they got back home, we began to plan their reception. Jason's plan was to keep the wedding a secret and have another wedding ceremony. I laid out a simpler plan: Announce that they got legally married in Las Vegas and would now be married before God in another wedding ceremony. He agreed and they were married by Pastor Tom Bauer in 2005 at the Hyatt Regency Waikiki.

Donna's whole family came as did relatives from across the country. The wedding was a big celebration with the Koreans outshining the locals. They were dressed in customary Korean dress. But Donna intensely missed her Dad. He had such a tough life and never got to see her marry. (figure 16, page 50)

A few days later, Donna had a dream: They were living in a condominium and her Dad came to visit. He brought a suitcase and sat down at their dining table. They talked and laughed and time stood still. But suddenly her father said, "I have to go." Donna pleaded, "Dad don't go!" Still, he picked up his suitcase, opened the front door, and left. As Donna looked out after him, she saw a beautiful garden with flowers and trees illuminated by bright sunlight. Donna realized God sent her time with her Dad. The suitcase symbolized the temporary nature of his visit and the garden and bright sunlight represented heaven, where her father is now. Donna knows that God sent her much-needed comfort.

GRANDMA'S DREAMS

My Mom has always had dreams and she's 90 years old. Now that she knows it is God who sends dreams, she's at peace knowing God always communicates with her. That makes her "weird" dreams less weird. It's also been a treat to interpret "Grandma's" dreams for her. She waits for me to come so she can tell me her dream. Sometimes it's a week or two before she remembers and shares. And it really doesn't make a lot of difference whether my interpretation is right or not. It fosters fun conversation, much-needed in her state of dementia. She's had visions of other people in her room besides her many caregivers. People call that "seeing things." I choose to believe God who says in the Last Days people will have dreams and visions. Mom chooses to believe God too.

My Dad was extremely disciplined. The Bible calls it self-control. At work, he was highly regarded by his employees but also highly feared. Even when he was angry and had to scold the men, he was in control. He strategically chose the ones upon whom he would unleash his controlled anger. It was all part of his correction to create memorable moments.

Dad was a Superman. I could never have done what he did to build a business from scratch. I'm a manager, but God used Dad to build the business so I would have people to manage. In the early days, he did all the estimating, negotiating, engineering, project management, administration, billing, and collection, and then his real day started: actual electrical installation. I don't know how he did it.

Once his business grew, he settled into what he considered the most important part of the business: estimating jobs, negotiating final contracts and customer relations. He would spend 80-90% of his day doing "takeoffs," all by longhand. A "takeoff" is to measure the quantity of materials from contract plans and then make an educated guess as to how many labor hours an electrician would take to install it. At best, a good estimator could be reasonably consistent, at worst it was a crapshoot.

I started working in the business in 1970 with a full head of hair. I gave much to the business, even the hair. Every so often Dad would invite me to lunch. It was always to the Inn of the Sixth Happiness, a great Chinese restaurant. He started work early so we could go to lunch by 11 a.m. When he was ready, he'd call on the intercom, "Okay, Junior, let's go to lunch." Dad and I share the same name, so it was settled early on that he would be "Senior" and I would be "Junior." People in the Hawaii construction biz still call me "Junior."

One night, in 2014, Grandma dreamt that Senior was on the intercom calling Jason, "Okay, Jason, let's go to lunch." The interpretation was clear: God was connecting Senior to my son. He was letting the Yamadas know that He had chosen Jason from birth to run the company. He had guided Jason all his years to entrust the company to him — all the workers, their families, the relationships developed over the whole construction industry over the past 60 plus years. God was confirming that I heard Him correctly. God was also confirming to Jason that He's in control, so Jason can trust Him. (P.S. Jason was the only grandchild Senior held in his arms, but he is not the only one he will hold in heaven.) (figure 17, page 51)

GRANDPA AGAIN

Mom had many dreams of Dad over the years — he appeared in her house and in her bedroom sitting on the floor. My sister Sharon remembers a dream Mom had where Dad came to visit. "In the dream, Mom took out her towels and laid them out because Dad was a special guest in her house." God showed Mom how much she loved Dad. (Still haven't figured out the towels.)

In September 2014, Mom dreamt she was looking for Dad's picture franticly and couldn't find it. (figure 18, page 51) When she finally found it, the picture "went up in *obake* (Japanese ghost) smoke." God showed her how precious her husband was to her. God took Dad on January 13, 1979. Mom has lived longer without him (35 years) than she did with him (33 years), but she still loves him. The concept of "obake smoke" is less clear. However, it is something Mom is familiar with as she has seen Japanese movies. Since God sent the dream, the use of smoke may signify God's involvement; He took Dad. Some aspects of any dream may remain unclear; we only get full clarification from God. The key is that He's communicating with Mom. That is 90% of the message of dreams, understanding is a bonus.

GRANDMA'S DREAM TO COMFORT US

Early in our ministry at Hawaii Cedar Church, God had us giving things away. Diana would write people's names on tickets and we would call them out before service. That person would receive a blessing.

One season we recognized that the homeless need phones to get employment. Whoever was trying to get a job and had filled out job applications could apply for a "boost phone." We gave them out after service in a lottery. One day we had a huge problem after most of our congregation left. One attendee was upset that he did not get a phone. He was 6'2", 250 pounds of solid man and towering over my sister Sharon. He began to get violent, yelling and swearing at her: "I deserve a phone!"

Our Security Officer, Lee, immediately got between the man and Sharon and asked him to leave. Lee escorted him out and watched him walk away. Still concerned for our safety, Lee checked the streets surrounding the church property to make sure he was not loitering nearby. He returned and said, "I went up and down, and looked all around; he's nowhere to be found."

That same night, Mom had a dream (retold by Sharon): "A man dressed in white was standing in her living room. She asked him what he was doing there and he replied, 'I came to see about a problem.' She was frightened so she ran to her neighbor Gerald's house. It was 4 a.m. and Gerald's mom came to the door. Mom explained the emergency, so Gerald went to check Mom's house. With a flashlight and his cell phone in hand, he went to look for the intruder. After checking her house and surrounding property, he told Mom, 'I went up and down, and looked all around; he's nowhere to be found.'"

Sharon was shocked; she had just heard those exact words from Lee. Mom then told Sharon that Gerald took out his cell phone and started showing her pictures of a dog. Skeptical, Sharon explained that Gerald would not do that at 4 a.m. She must've been dreaming. Mom insisted she was not dreaming, Gerald really did come to her house, and the man had come to see her about a problem.

This discussion happened while they were driving home. So Sharon told Mom that if God wanted her to talk to Gerald, then Gerald will be outside of his home. Lo and behold! As Sharon turned onto Mom's street, Gerald was out by his car. So Sharon pulled up. Gerald verified it all, he had actually gone to Mom's house at 4 a.m. Bewildered, Sharon asked why he would show pictures of a dog at such a time. Gerald replied, "We were both awake already and I know your Mom loves dogs."

It was then that Sharon made a connection to what happened at church. At service I had used a flashlight to represent God's Light. Gerald had held both a flashlight and a cell phone, the two items that represented church that day. Sharon saw God's Hand and found comfort that He is with us.

Sharon knew God sent that dream and orchestrated events to confirm that we were on track at Hawaii Cedar Church. Even so, we hired a policeman. We trust God in the mission, but also firmly believe He gave us authorities in the flesh. Cedar AOG now has a group of BIG security men.

6

FRIENDS' DREAMS

DOOR OF FAITH: MILDRED BROSTEK

The luminous legacy of **Door of Faith Church** was launched by one woman: **Mildred Brostek**. As a young girl, Mildred was called by God during the Great Depression from Georgia via Florida to Hawaii. She had a very tough life. Ma and Pa Johnson had 10 children. In the mid-30's Ma, Mildred's sister, and her husband went from Florida to Burbank, California. Theirs was a simple plan: Work hard, save money, and send for the rest of the family, two by two, until eventually they could all be together again. Mildred Johnson (her maiden name) had life-threatening pneumonia as a teen and almost died. God came to her in a vision and told her He was sending her to "a faraway land with palm trees and with brown-skinned people whom she would later love." She asked, "Why me?" As she accepted His plan, God healed her. She graduated from Holmes Bible College and her family scraped together the funds to send her to Hawaii in 1936.

Mildred traveled to the tiny, remote island of Molokai. While walking the plank from her vessel, a cattle ship, to the dingy that would take her ashore, she dropped her purse into the bay. It was all she had, and her family would not be able to help. Hawaii is legendary for its aloha, after all we are the "Aloha State," and a Molokai family took her in. God soon provided sufficient funds for her return to Honolulu. In 1937, Mildred founded the **First Pentecostal Holiness Mission** by opening a modest storefront right in central Honolulu. Shortly after, she met her husband, **Alexander Peter Brostek**.

According to their church website: "Despite much ridicule from her colleagues because of her gender, with poise and determination [Mildred] ministered to her first flock: 'a motley crew of kids from the neighborhood.' She eventually moved the church to Pauoa Valley near the old ice factory and later to Kalihi.… In 1940 she established the **Door of Faith Church and Bible School** which led the way in popularizing a fundamental view of Christianity in the isles." (Figure 19 and Figure 20, page 52)

GOD CONNECTS PEOPLE, JUST LOOK FOR HIS HAND

The saying "It's a small world" is true because we have a BIG GOD. When I read that Pastor Mildred had established her mission at 1988 Pauoa Road it was intriguing that my path would cross with hers. My mom grew up not 100 yards away, in a small camp by "Ice Mill." I grew up in Pauoa Valley and when I walked home from school, I passed by that location every day (although they had moved by then).

I first met her son, **Alexander Peter Brostek Jr.**, when I got a call for electrical work for their flagship church on Young Street. We arranged to meet, spent about 30 minutes, I gave him a ballpark estimate and we were off and running. I assigned one of our Project Managers to the job and didn't think much of it. However, God forged a stronger connection. Peter thought our company had saved them a ton of money so he called to thank me. Actually, God was moving on Peter's heart to give me favor as He connected us for a continuing journey that He had planned.

We started meeting regularly to discuss construction issues but we also connected as men of God. We had a lot in common: We were both "Junior," we both went to Roosevelt High, both were "bad boys" growing up (Peter was worse), and we both had a wild side.

Peter is a dinosaur in good ways and some not-so-good. He doesn't carry a cellphone, never used a computer and, as such, never needed the Internet. He used a whiteboard. One day, at Yanagi Sushi, music came up and he told me he loved Bob Dylan. I love Bob! So I whipped out my iPhone and played some songs; made him jealous. (Best way to take a guy to the next level.)

We talked about the cool things that an iPhone and even a computer (gasp!) can do. Within a week I got an e-mail from Peter! He'd gone out and bought himself a touch-screen computer. God used Dylan to get Peter connected to cyberspace. It was a part of His future plan. It started as a means of trustworthy communication — Peter didn't always answer his phone. Worse, he didn't always check his message machine. But with his "new-fangled fascination," Peter was hooked, at least on e-mail.

PETER'S FIRST DREAM

Peter was systematic in our meetings, always carrying a yellow note-pad with notes to "report." He would list everything we previously discussed and then update me with a follow-up. And he always did what he said he would do. In fact, Peter always moved three steps forward (although, occasionally, two steps back!) by keeping his focus on Jesus. On Tuesday **August 16, 2011**, we were at a favorite meeting spot, Stage Restaurant. He was under intense pressure. I try to never give advice as my model is not what I think is right, but "What is God thinking?" or "What is God doing?" And, as most people do, Peter came to his own conclusion. I asked if he ever had dreams. Peter said he rarely did and didn't believe God spoke that way today.

I challenged him to ask God for dreams. The next day, I got this e-mail (verbatim):

Agape
Bro Jimmy
On Wed, Aug 17, 2011 at 4:13 AM, Peter Brostek wrote:

"good morning jimmy! Dream.....i am driving alone in a convertible sports car after a terrible storm....driving up a winding road like Tantalus drive...obstacles like fallen trees, abandoned vehicles and power lines are all over the road...carefully i avoid running into objects and continue on....finally after a real tight hairpin turn i reach the top of the mountain where there is a parking lot and a multi-storied building....debris is everywhere....i see no one. I park and i'm approaching the facility looking any sign of life or people....END (OF DREAM)

"I see many signs here but only care of this----the ABSOLUTE knowledge i have that GOD LOVES me, LOVES me...and sees me through in spite of my reckless and contrary ways....tired of being physically alone however. I don't care much for this dream stuff. we will talk later. We are BLESSED!!"

---------- Forwarded message ----------
From: Jr Yamada
Date: Wednesday, August 17, 2011
Subject: Dream
To: Peter Brostek
Cc: Jimmy Yamada

HUGE
Dreams are sent from God. While only God can interpret dreams, the foundation he uses is the Bible. You've heard it said: Let the Bible interpret the Bible. Well, also, the Bible is the way to understand dreams from God.

One of the neat things with dreams from God, is that you can hear from HIM clearly (once you understand HIS message-which is not often clear).

One of the spooky things is that now that something is clear, we have no excuse for not obeying.

(OOPS... I forgot to tell you about that part)

Here's how I see your dream:

"Driving is usually life path… on your (God) journey.

Sports convertible car speaks of the fast, reckless, untamed lifestyle in your past.

Storm speaks of storms, but it's past, so you have passed the past storms (we never stop going thru storms).

Winding road, uphill—life's journey for us is a winding journey and it's an uphill battle (already won).

You seem to be now moving thru life carefully, avoiding fallen trees, abandoned vehicles (other people's abandoned paths), you are bypassing carefully "dangerous power lines"—fallen power (evil?)

Tight hairpin turn—you have taken a sharp radical quick detour in the past 2 years. New direction.

At the top parking lot with multi-storied bldg, debris everywhere, no one there—This is where Door of Faith is now, empty bldgs with lots of parking—lots of capacity for new people, for new life. Not many in Door of Faith understand this, so God is showing you what you felt yesterday at lunch—you stand alone, like John the Baptist, Daniel, Joseph, Moses… your mom when she first got here.

You park and you walk towards the facility—Keep walking—you are right, God will guide you, God will empower you, He loves you. You are not alone… Holy Spirit is living in you, Jesus is interceding for you as He sits at the right hand of God, and the Father is looking down at you…

And Jimmy is praying for you and is with you... You are not alone. I am here with you, in the spirit."

Peter asked God to speak to him in a dream and God answered. Peter realized a few things from the dream immediately after he awoke:

1. God had sent him a dream after he asked for it.
2. God revealed to Peter that He knew what Peter was going through.
3. Peter knew the dream was exactly what was going on.
4. Peter couldn't see the end, but **he was comforted that God knew and was with Him**. Peter drew strength even though his difficulties didn't go away.

GOD: "PETER NEVER ABANDONS HIS PEOPLE"

On **January 17, 2012**, Peter had another dream and shared it with me: "Part 1 — In a big construction yard. I'm working with floor plans and reflected ceiling plans, 3-dimensional, huge yard...there are cranes in the center of the yard. Cranes are holding up a 3-dimensional model of a building. I'm signaling the guy who is in the air and controlling the crane. I'm directing the crane operator that something is wrong and that he should bring back the right one (model).

Part 2 — Setting is a War Zone, like Iraq. I have in front on me a huge tablecloth. One man cannot carry it. I walk out into a big open space, like a green zone (in military terms, a green zone is a safe zone). While in big open space, I unroll the tablecloth on the ground. I see a fighting vehicle with troops, a Humvee with a trailer. Humvee drives up the middle and the tablecloth picks up and flies away, like a magic carpet, then comes back. While the carpet and men are gone, I feel a gut-wrenching apprehension, a fear of loss. The tablecloth flies back with the men and equipment, but the men are wounded and busted up. I run alongside the tablecloth as it comes to a stop.

Our joint interpretation:

Part 1 — Peter was educated as an architect but his expertise was as a builder. God confirmed that. Peter always improved upon whatever the architects had designed. It's difficult to draw up every detail and condition, especially in the old days, but Peter's forte was making the details work flawlessly.

Part 2 — God revealed that much of Peter's life was a war zone. He was still going through a storm in ministry and personal life. The tablecloth represented the supernatural power of God. God was always there, but Peter would always try to do things on his own. (Peter cannot carry the tablecloth). He could fix things like architectural details, but not God-sized church issues. When Peter entered the safe zone—God's zone—he can unroll the tablecloth. This was significant: Peter was starting to trust God.

The Humvee with troops show that God saw Peter among the troops in the battle. Once Peter depended on God, the tablecloth flew away then returned. While the men are gone, Peter sensed a gut-wrenching apprehension; his precise situation in early 2012. The tablecloth returned with the men busted up. Others had been caught in the turmoil, yet Peter kept "running alongside" his people. He never abandoned them. We realized later that the people in the ministry did return after the battle was over. But at that time, all we knew was that Peter was remaining faithful and God was showing His approval.

God knew exactly what Peter was going through and that brought peace and strength.

DREAM: PETER HEADED FOR A TELEPHONE POLE

Here's an e-mail from Peter received on **April 17, 2012**:
"Bro. Jimmy,
I did not get home until 7pm last night....right to bed...
Hope I can see you today....let me know whatever.

Vivid dream I had Sunday night (15th):

I'm driving a CAR on flat landscape (road).

There are now people in vehicle with me.

Don't know who they are....maybe you and Jesus!

As I'm driving I'm heading straight for a telephone pole (power pole). I try to step on the brake, but there is a tangled mesh of extension cord under my feet.

As I step on the brake pedal, the tangled mesh also presses down on the gas pedal at the same time.

This malfunction locks the steering and I cannot turn away from the telephone pole.

Eventually I am able to bring the car to a stop just short of the pole and collision.

With the vehicle stopped, the steering unlocks and I turn the car (left) back to the center of roadway.

This exact dream repeats 3 times...and I wake up.

Let me know about today...Peter-dono" [Peter meant "domo"- arigato, or Japanese for thanks.)

Interpretation:

1. "Car on flat landscape": Level ground means things are not bad, versus first dream was a steep upward climb and things were rough. Also, first was a sports car, now a regular car. The old Peter was fast-moving and now he is more stable.

2. "People are now in the car": Peter is not alone.

3. "Headed straight for a telephone pole": Peter is headed for a crash and not out of the woods yet.

4. "Step on brake...presses gas pedal at same time": Peter was not in control; God was in control.

5. "Steering wheel cannot turn": God emphasized that only He could change the course Peter was on.

6. "Eventually stop...car pointed to center": God stopped and corrected situation, through Peter's hands.

7. The dream repeats three times, a Biblical principle: *"The reason the dream was given to Pharaoh in **two forms** is that the matter has been firmly decided by God, and God will do it soon"* (Gen. 41:32).

By this time, Peter and I were meeting weekly and having a grand time. Peter recognized that God was the sender of dreams. It became clear then (and even clearer now) that God revealed what was to take place in Peter's life and that He was in control. Now, as we look back in hindsight, we can see how the dreams came true over the past 2½ years. God gave us the "big picture" then, but today it's crystal clear.

GOD ORCHESTRATES LOVE

Peter had a difficult time with women in his life, first his mother and then his wife. Peter's legendary mother, Mildred, was anointed by God for a great work but she was not a great parent. It was similar to some of God's greatest men in the Bible. Case in point: Samuel. His sons went so far off-track that they engaged in a sex scandal and embezzlement right in God's temple! (And under their father's nose.) Similarly, my friend Peter did not experience the best parenting and he too lead a wild life in his early years.

Consequently, Peter and his wife divorced 30 years ago. She passed away in 2014. However, Peter chose to live a life pleasing to God no matter how hard the challenges in ministry or in his personal life. A few years ago, Peter desired (God-inspired) to have a female partner. Now that he was Internet-savvy, he started searching for a new life companion. Peter was looking for an Asian woman, preferably Japanese. "Over the years at Door of Faith," Peter shared, "God provided many surrogate mothers and fathers of Japanese descent to take care of me. They were some of the early solid supporters of the church." God used that Japanese connection to connect him to his future wife. (And me!)

So Peter spent a few years pouring over a website connecting with women. Whenever Peter got a little serious about one of them, I would get a "report." One day he told me he may have found "the one." She was Vietnamese, in her late 50s and had come from Vietnam as one of the "boat people." She raised her kids alone and they were all educated and successful in their careers. Peter went to visit her and meet her family. Her kids were suspicious at first, but realized he wasn't a gigolo.

Peter shared a dream he then had (late 2011): "I'm standing in an outdoor setting. A (Vietnamese) woman is standing next to me and we're both standing outside a huge garden courtyard. In front of us are two big columns like in an Egyptian temple. Just as we are both getting ready to walk through the entry towards the garden, I hear God's voice really distinct: 'I am orchestrating this relationship.' I turn back to see who was talking (although I knew it had to be God) and then I woke up."

Interpretation: God was telling Peter this lady friend was not the right one. He knew God was in control. Within months, God brought a few other Japanese women into his life. None were right. At the same time, God brought another guy to our group, **Pastor John Rogers**, of the Assemblies of God.

The first time Peter mentioned **Ritsuko**, we were having lunch at Sizzlers. He showed John and I a picture, and we both snapped to and took notice. (figure 21, page 53) When did this happen? Peter beamed, a Brostek revelation: he'd been keeping her a secret. The picture was from months earlier in Summer 2012.

Peter started to get serious with "Ritzi," as he lovingly called her, a play on the "ritzy, classy" lady he saw in her. He eventually went to

Japan to meet her family. He told her he wasn't interested in seeing Japan's sights, he simply wanted to spend time with her and her family, including a visit to her deceased father's grave site. He considered it a great honor to accompany Ritzi to visit her father.

Peter and Ritzi were married on October 26, 2013. I had the honor of officiating the wedding. (figure 22, page 53) God had certainly orchestrated their relationship and Peter was ecstatic to be led by the Hand of God. A few months ago, Peter told me about yet an earlier dream with Ritzi...

"MOUNTAIN MAN PETE"

Peter shared a dream (mid 2014): "I was a giant mountain that towered high above the terrain below. I was aware that I was a mountain but not aware that I had legs, hands and feet. I had eyes and could see, and as I started moving, I looked around at the landscape. I thought to myself, 'I think I'll go out to the sea.' I walked into the ocean, which was very deep, but I (as the mountain) am not submerged. I go deeper and deeper and reach a place in the ocean where I decide to sit. I'm half in the water and half above the water (like Mauna Kea).

"I feel the ocean is so comfortable and cool and I enjoy sitting in it. I'm suddenly aware that I have hands and look down and see a whale. I pet the whale with my left hand and the dream ends."

When he shared his dream with Ritzi, she told him of a scuba encounter. She had one of her deepest, most powerful religious experiences in her life: She came within six feet of a whale. Awe-inspiring!

God's communication is multi-faceted and has deeper, intimate meanings. In this dream, God was connecting Peter and Ritzi spiritually as soulmates through a similar experience. An added note: Peter was never an ocean guy; Ritzi always enjoyed the ocean. God showed Peter that whatever Ritzi enjoys, he will enjoy, which is why the ocean was "so comfortable." God gave them that "moment" as a gift. The dream wouldn't make sense to Peter until Ritzi revealed her reality in the same moment.

God continues to orchestrate their love. Peter is the happiest he's ever been in his life. When we three disciples — Peter, James and John — get together, we notice that Peter can't stop smiling.

JORDAN SENG: A MIRACLE WORKER (figure 23, page 54)

Pastor Jordan Seng is a highly-anointed servant in God's Kingdom. He could have been a movie actor yet is a most charismatic, down-to-earth pastor. He speaks softly and carries a huge message. God called him to plant **Bluewater Mission Church**. Dr. Seng holds degrees from Stanford University and the University of Chicago, with a Ph.D. in Political Theory. Dr. Seng is a doer not a talker (though he is a great preacher). He has authored a world-famous book, "Miracle Work": "It's one thing to accept that supernatural stuff happens; it's another thing to accept it when it happens; it's still another thing to be the one through whom it happens… God routinely partners with us to get things done in the world. He reveals truth, but we have to preach it." [1]

Three of his dream experiences standout to me from his book. Believe it or not they started as a child: "I had a number of predictive dream experiences when I was a child, but since I didn't know any Christians who claimed to hear from God in dreams or visions, I wrote off most of my experiences (or tried not to think about them too much)." One included a graphic and detailed description of the then-upcoming Sugar Ray Leonard and Roberto Durán boxing match. It was just before Dr. Seng turned 13 years of age and he could see the boxers' trunks, the colors they wore, even the declared winner, which was the underdog, Durán. What the young Seng learned wasn't that God needed him to start gambling on sports events, but to start banking his eternity on the Author of Dreams, the Living God. From then forward Seng started paying attention to his dreams and was able to learn how prophetic they were. Later he became a pastor of his own church and perked up when five or six members started having similar dreams about unspeakable things being done to women and children. They realized it was the breaking wave of human trafficking in Hawaii, and they knew God was asking them to do something about it. Because Pastor Jordan was attuned to God's dreams, Bluewater Mission took necessary action. Pastor Jordan shares many more dreams, in his book, "Miracle Work." Read it; it's inspiring!

JOHN ROGERS' VISION

John and Pat Rogers have been through a lot. Or rather, John put Pat through a lot! (figure 24, page 55) John graduated from Aiea High and figured out the fastest way to success: work three full-time jobs. **Live fast, die young!** Of course with that schedule, his wife and family were left in the dust.

By the mid-90s, John had a solid six-digit income working for Motorola's Asian Region. His operation base was in Japan and he had luxurious living quarters fit for a little emperor. However, in 1998, God got ahold of John's heart. They left their comfortable lifestyle and landed at **First Assembly of God**.

Promotion comes from God and He put John on the fast track — from teaching to administration and finally into a pastoral role. One day his seventh-grade class was giggling behind John's back, calling him, "Pastor John." He replied, "I know why you're laughing." They said, "No, you don't." Curious, John called them on it. They replied, "We know you're a pastor and you don't." Out of the mouths of babes!

John became executive pastor at FAOG and assisted Pastor Klayton Ko. At an all-night prayer in October 2011, God sent John a vision. This is his recollection of the vision and succeeding events:

"Vision: At the altar lost in worship and prayer, my eyes look up! Jesus is standing over me. He points to 3 doors and tells me to choose one: 'One will cost little, one will cost much, and one will cost everything!' I ask if He can help me make the choice and start crying. I take my eyes off of Him. When I look up there is one Door. Pointing to it, He says this is the door for me. I start crying again and He is gone.

That night: I continue worshiping Him at the altar with deep sobs. I was asked to share the vision to all present by the Service Leader.

Pastor John also shared the events that ensued afterwards: "Three weeks later I was asked by a friend if I would ever consider leaving First Assembly. I was caught off-guard but considering the Vision (which was still resonating in my Spirit) I said, 'I can't say no.'

"Two weeks later, that friend invited me to have breakfast with a friend of his. It was Pastor Peter Brostek. We immediately hit it off. Three months later, Pastor Peter asked me to consider the position of Senior Pastor of Door of Faith Church and Bible School.

"After two more months of prayer and discussion," John shared, "I accepted, believing that this was the DOOR that Jesus had chosen for me." John was installed on September 1, 2012. He was part of God's Hand bringing relief to Pastor Peter Brostek and the Door of Faith Church.

GOD GUIDES MISSY

Cedar Assembly of God is our home church, a new family whom God is building. God brought Pastor Darrick and Missy Nakata as a perfect fit — they love God and God guides them with dreams.

They've been separated from their daughter, **Mia**, for about seven years. (Unable to travel to Las Vegas due to a parole violation.) This has been extremely difficult, especially for Missy, but God had a plan: Time to grow Darrick and Missy spiritually, emotionally, and mentally. They needed time to clean up and God knew they needed years. He was working for their ultimate good, not just a short-term firework show. Meanwhile, Mia was 15 years old when Mom and Dad left, so she grew up with **Grandma Gerri**. Mia stayed on the straight-and-narrow growing up Catholic. She had a strong relationship with God.

God sent Missy a dream: "Our family was driving on a freeway and had pulled over. Darrick and I got out and were walking away while Mia stayed. Suddenly, I heard a screeching sound. I looked back and saw a semi with a container had jack-knifed and rolled over our car. There was nothing left."

The dream horrified Missy. However, dreams must be interpreted within context. Otherwise, what God intends as a blessing can create fear. And that was the case with Missy's dream. She feared her daughter was going to get into a car crash and be crushed.

A month after the dream, God blessed the Nakatas with a bargain on a car for Mia. They had saved for two years. But once they bought the car, Missy was anxious and filled with fear. Soon after, Missy felt the Lord correct her: The dream was not about an accident; it was actually about her as a mother crushing Mia with her love. She was always "on her kid's case." In fact, when they bought the car, Missy wanted Mia to sign a contract promising to finish college. Would you sign a contract like that?!

Once Missy recognized what God was revealing—that she was impeding Mia's spiritual growth—life changed for the better. Missy thanks God for His enlightenment. Although she may never be "healed" of being a mother, she knows Who to go to for help: Jesus.

This was an important dream for Missy. God had to make sure Missy got the message so He controlled the clarity, content and timing. He also made sure it was so graphic that Missy would vividly remember the dream. That way she would not let go of it until she got interpretation and changed. By the way, Mia was already 21 and very responsible; but, of course, God knew that.

¹ Seng, Jordan. 2013. *Miracle Work: A Down-to-Earth Guide to Supernatural Ministries*. Downers Grove, IL. InterVarsity Press.

7

GOD IS SURE; ARE YOU?

"The bride belongs to the bridegroom.
The friend who attends the bridegroom waits and listens for him,
and is full of joy when he hears the bridegroom's voice.
That joy is mine, and it is now complete.
He must become greater; I must become less."
(John 3:29-30)

There's no doubt that God speaks to us in dreams, the real question:
Are we listening?

As we conclude this book, we know that God speaks in many ways. Over 90% of the time it's through His Word. We also hear His voice in our hearts — through our spouses, circumstances and more. Those who hear Him best are those who love Him most and obey. I'm not in that category; I'm slow to hear and stubborn to obey. Thank God for grace.

Mother Teresa heard God's audible voice when He called her to the Missionaries of Charity: "Mother Teresa was actually hearing Jesus' voice and intimately conversing with Him. She is among those saints to whom Jesus spoke directly, asking them to undertake a special mission among His people. From the beginning of this extraordinary experience Mother Teresa had no doubt that it was Jesus who was speaking to her." (Kolodiejchuk, 2007) The biographer captures a poignant quote from Teresa: "Yet the 'Voice' kept pleading, 'Come, come, carry Me into the homes of the poor. Come, be My light.' Jesus' invitation was imbued with trust; He counted on her response." [1]

Once she started the Missionaries of Charity, she never heard His voice again. It was her greatest disappointment. I'd be a fool to assume I may know why Jesus stopped audibly communicating with Mother Teresa. But I am foolish, so I'll venture a thought: God had so much faith in her He didn't need to guide her audibly. He knew she would finish the task He set in front of her. Most of us need constant guidance and reassurance to know He is with us, especially in difficult times.

Diana's Leahi Hospital gang thinks of her as Mother Teresa. She's a steadfast, solid server. I'm a thinker. Diana doesn't have many dreams. She knows what she loves to do, serving, and does it. I think she over-serves. She says I over-think. She thinks everyone should simply serve. Can she be wrong? Jesus came to serve, so maybe He doesn't think she over-serves. Maybe Jesus doesn't have to send her too many dreams because He doesn't want her to change. She doesn't need His constant encouragement to keep going. I do. I'm a wimp. Dreams encourage me in my journey. I know the Bible, but I'm weak. Maybe you are too. If you're seeking God, then asking Him to guide you through dreams helps. This concluding chapter will deal with a few polishing principles to that end.

HEARING: WHEN SOMETHING
MEANINGFUL IS AT STAKE (figure 25, page 55)

Growing up in the 1950s, God incubated me in Pauoa Valley like He did the Hebrews in Egypt. It was my safe haven, even if the Papakolea (Hawaiian homestead) Boys played in Booth Park. They didn't pick on us, possibly because we were too little and of no consequence to them. I remember playing at the park with my friends at the tender age of seven. Today few parents allow that, unsupervised.

My Dad came home from work around 5:30 p.m. and dinner would be served promptly. My Mom was my alarm clock: She'd go to the back bedroom window overlooking the valley to call, "Jimmy Boy, come home!" She'd call me once and I would have five minutes to get home. I immediately stopped whatever I was doing and ran through the park, up one street, across Booth Road, through the Silva's yard, over the fence, through the Uyetake's yard, up their driveway, and be in the kitchen to eat dinner. The key was "hearing" her voice. If I missed that, an immediate "super chai" awaited me. I always heard her, clearly. Sadly, I don't always hear the voice of my Lord Jesus. Maybe it's because a "super chai" doesn't await me. Dreams play an important part in hearing His voice. Tune in!

LEARNING FACTORS: MONEY ON LINE &
TIME RUNNING OUT

One great motivator, more like human jet propulsion, is "money is on the line" aka something important at stake. In our early years, it's studying for a test, especially finals. Concentration levels peak at these times and makes for solid retention and strong analysis. Working at A-1, concentration was best when we were working on a bid for a large project. Our teams would work for months to put everything together and on the day we had to submit our final proposal, an unreal adrenalin rush kicked in. It helped me to remember numbers and similar projects that would aid in the current project. I now know God was there, even pre-Christ. The larger the project, the more intense the day. And the day before the final deadline was nowhere as intense as the last hour. The last 10 minutes even more so.

Allow me to quantum leap: **I hear from God best when I realize the stakes are HUGE and the time is SHORT.** The stakes are the highest because it's about souls. And the time is very short!

"EARS TO HEAR": DESIRE IS KEY

Jesus said: *"This is why I speak to them in parables: Though seeing, they do not see; though hearing, they do not hear or understand. In them is fulfilled the prophecy of Isaiah: 'You will be ever hearing but never understanding; you will be ever seeing but never perceiving. For this **people's heart has become calloused**; they hardly hear with their ears, and they have closed their eyes. Otherwise they might see with their eyes, hear with their ears, understand with their hearts and turn, and I would heal them.' But blessed are your eyes because they see, and your ears because they hear. For I tell you the truth, many prophets and righteous men longed to see what you see but did not see it, and to hear what you hear but did not hear it."* (Matthew 13:13-17)

We may apply this concept to dreams: Only those with a sincere desire to hear, will hear. One might assume that anyone who is born-again will hear, but I disagree. Many don't want what God wants. Example: If God wanted me to go to Africa and I don't want to. The problem is I'm a "buffet Christian," picking what I like from God's feast of life. While that works well at Tsukiji Market Restaurant (a great buffet), it's not effective in God's Kingdom. It shows God that I'm still in control, not Him; I'm Lord of my life.

Let's take that concept a little further: Since I don't want to go to Africa, my dreams will never be interpreted in the light of Africa. It's "off my radar." The same happened once when we took our serving team to Tsukiji Market and I didn't see the ribs or shrimp tempura. I didn't see it because I wasn't looking for it as I had no desire to eat it. Be open to God's delicacies and you'll begin to dream brighter and broader dreams.

PRIDE: THE ROADBLOCK TO HEARING

In his classic "Mere Christianity," C.S. Lewis wrote: "The essential vice, the utmost evil, is Pride. Unchastity, anger, greed, drunkenness, and all that, are mere fleabites in comparison: it was through Pride that the devil became the devil: Pride leads to every other vice. It is the complete anti-God state of mind." [2]

C.S. Lewis hit a bullseye. And God has spent a good deal of time working on my wretched pride. Diana often says, "You only *think* you know everything." Paul wrote that if you think you know, you dunno.

In business, God allowed A-1 A-Lectrician to prosper, and then to falter. When we almost went broke in 1977-1978, my pride shriveled. It grew again from 1980-1984 when A-1 did well. In 1985 when A-1 hit a speed bump, it shriveled a bit, but then grew from 1986-1991 when we did well again. When I was born again on June 6, 1993, I became aware of my pride. Diana helped.

In 2003, A-1 had another difficult period, and again God humbled me lovingly. I had already seen how great a sinner I was in my first 45 years, but obviously God was not done with me yet. He used our business to get my attention as it was still the most important thing to me and defined who I was, even as a Christian. Pride doesn't disappear just because we're born again. God deals with our pride because it is a great sin and because it keeps us from hearing Him. As such, pride preempts dreams.

PRIDE & MY WIFE: A DEADLY COMBINATION

After coming to Jesus, God shifted my focus to my wife Diana and my family. I resolved to love her in a way that pleased the Lord. It dawned upon me that Diana is God's child. **Duh!** I needed to allow her to grow into the person He desired. So I made it a goal to not force my ideas upon her. After 20 years, I'm at about 30%; still far to go. If I get there, my pride will surely balloon.

I tried to allow Diana freedom to voice her thoughts and feelings without being a "baby monster" and dominating her. I would do that by complaining. However, as I healed from being a baby monster, I became a logic monster. I call this progress. Diana feels it's more of the same. Over the last 10 years (takes time for old guys), God slowly healed me of being a logic monster too.

One "revelation moment" from God happened when Diana and I were talking about Daven. My logic was Biblical but it still made me a monster: "Why are you thinking evil about my son?" Diana got angry, threw down her spoon, flew her dishes in the sink, and walked out. I quickly apologized, told her I loved her, and said, "I'm wrong." God spoke clearly to me: *"Do I want to be right or righteous?"*

In her anger, Diana told me that I always try to control her. *Say, what?!* I realized that it's not about what I *think*, but what she *feels*. God was still working on my pride. It's always there, lurking. It never completely disappears, but I believe we can tame it, like our tongue. When we do, we hear more clearly from God.

PASTORS GROUPS

Another event at the same time happened with my pastors group. I pushed too hard to get the group to move in a direction that I wanted. Again, God dealt with my pride: "You don't know everything; and you don't know what I want for this group."

On **May 20, 2014** I had a three-part dream. First part: "Pastor Ko is teaching something."

Second part: "I'm showering using a water hose in the front parking area outside, naked except for a small hand towel over my privates."

Third part: "There was a truck with the engine out (hood open). I'm checking the engine. Seems rusting. Engine block on the exterior of car."

Interpretation: First, Pastor Ko was my pastor for my first 14 years and I still consider him to be my pastor. I go to him in major situations. God is telling me I need to listen and learn more, not just push my ideas on everyone (wife, other leaders, etc.).

Second, clearly I need more humility. Nothing is more embarrassing than being publicly naked. God said, "If you're naked in front people, you will not speak, preach or teach. You'll be too embarrassed. Be quiet, sit down, and hope no one sees or hears you!"

Third, I know nothing about cars, engines, or anything that goes on under a car hood. God showed me that I have no business looking under the hood of that car.

God sent a dream to deal with my pride. My third book ("God's Hand in the Life of a Pastor") and this book are a direct result of God dealing with my pride and humbling me. He said it's better to write and let people decide what they want to digest. He'll work, I can rest; then I'll hear Him better.

GRACE: GOD WORKED IT ALL TOGETHER OVER 30 YEARS

As I look back over how God has spoken to me through our business (since the 70s!), through Diana, through other pastors and through my dreams, the theme is **God's grace**. Patiently He started in 1978 using the ups and downs of business to break through my calloused heart and weed out a small measure of pride. He also worked through someone I love more than anyone else in the world (except Jesus), Diana. He had her wait patiently. But He also had her finally explode to dig a little deeper in my heart. He further worked through fellow brothers. Then he sent a dream that I could clearly hear.

It would be foolish to say I heard His voice because I desired it. God was forced to work by grace so my ears would be open to hear. My pride had to be crippled. At a certain point, I stopped resisting and my heart became more open to Him. If I had remained the Jimmy Yamada, Jr. of the '80s, President and Dictator, I would surely have been deaf. (And dead. But again, thank God for grace!)

DREAMS SHOW HE IS WITH US

I must emphasize that I don't wait for dreams to know God's will at any moment. Yet God does send dreams within the context of life events. Like the May 20 dream, that would have been impossible to interpret had God not already been working for 30 years on my pride. My wife was patient with me and my faults. God made her strong so she could stand strong with me through it all. When she finally "blew up," it was completely outside of normal. In fact, she's only done that twice in the past 10 years.

Chapter 2 covered types of dreams and God's methods, all for guiding our walk with Him. For most, it is often difficult to hear His voice with all the noise of our lives. Especially when it gets busy. Yet we know that God is causing all things to work together for our good, and He is always communicating with us. The tricky part is to fit the correct communication into the right application, like a puzzle. Just think, it's a personal communique from Jesus Himself! John the Baptist's joy was from hearing Jesus' voice. Was that because he had a boring life? Or had nothing better to do? No, John the Baptist was to announce the coming Messiah and he had heard the fulfillment of that call! God's voice is exciting beyond belief!

We each have the anointed privilege of announcing Jesus Christ to someone. We have the honor of shining His light. We have the favor of knowing that when we go in His name, He goes with us and will never leave us. That power shows up in many different ways, one way is in dreams. The point is we should have the same joy as John the Baptist: *We have heard His voice!*

Most dreams are "talk story" (in fact they're meaningless to others). But what is tremendous is that God is talking with us! He's involved in every part of our lives! The takeaway is that we get to see His Hand, hear His voice, and sense His pleasure. And that is the greatest reward.

LIVING LIFE WITH CHRIST IN DREAMLAND

I'm still a young Christian, 21 years old as I write this. Because I got saved later in life, God took that "disadvantage" and turned it into an advantage: When I read the Bible I took it literally. Early on, this lead to a few debacles: I was an overzealous fundamentalist aka "wacko." As I shared the Gospel in the construction industry, on the street, while surfing, or anywhere, I got carried away. People sat sweating though my presentations. Yet I thought if I gave 100 reasons for believing God and the Gospel, people would come to Christ. My apologies if you were one of my "victims"!

The Biblical message that God speaks through dreams is one I took literally and I was not disappointed. However, it would be a mistake to focus on the dreams and not on the One who sends them. **The point of God speaking in dreams is to focus on God**. John the Baptist's joy was in hearing the voice of Jesus; his focus was not the voice, but Jesus!

God knows we need to focus on Him at all times. So it is with dreams, they help us to stay focused on Him. It's living life with Christ in Dreamland. Life is an up-and-down journey; dreams help to stabilize that squiggly line. Scripture promises He's with us, but when He shows up in dreams it's HUGE! Just think if Jesus were to appear to me in person, put His arms around me, look into my eyes and tell me something, it would blow my mind! In '60s lingo, it'd be "far out"! The impact on my soul is eternal and it affects my daily walk. He fulfills His name, "Immanuel," God is with us! Dreams have helped me to develop, to deepen my relationship with Him, and to pump up my passion.

PRAYER IS THE KEY

"In his heart a man plans his course, but the Lord determines his steps." (Proverbs 16:9)

If we want to receive God's "signals" for our steps, we need to be moving forward on His mission. That's the key: Being in the "zone" or place to hear Him clearly. Then all the distracting "noise" of life is filtered out. Prayer is the starting point: Ask God and await His answer. Typically, when we pray, we're the most sensitive to hearing from God. It's like surfing: You can't learn it from books and videos. The only way to learn to surf is to surf. Likewise, the best way to hear His "signals" is to walk with Him. As I look back upon my journey, I see that each step of the way I simply had to take one step: the first one. Every day another "first step" opportunity presented itself. I say "first," because God directed me daily, so the next step became another first step. I'm still taking first steps and I pray my last "first step" is into heaven. [3]

Eric Metaxas wrote in his book on the Nazi infiltrator, Bonhoeffer, "His thinking [was] that Christians cannot be governed by mere principles. Principles could carry one only so far. At some point every person must **hear from God**, must know what God was calling him to do, apart from others."

Bonhoeffer had a clear mission God revealed at the start of the war: to take out Hitler and hence the Nazis. Life prior to that was all preparation for his ultimate mission and prelude to becoming like Jesus. Some may think he failed as he died without seeing Hitler assassinated or overthrown and without seeing the German Church rise up. However, I believe **his greatest success was in becoming like Jesus.** His mission served to help him hear clearly and become more like God's Son.

Why would God send Bonhoeffer on a mission only to fail its "goals"? Because the mission was just a part of God's greater accomplishment in him: His legacy and witness for all of us and for all time. Everyone's ultimate goal is to become like Jesus: to hear clearly everything the Father says, to see everything though His eyes, and to **obey**. Success can only be measured through the Father's eyes. Therefore, those who do not have a clearly defined mission will have a more difficult time hearing from God. Dreams, their interpretation and revelation will be difficult because the context will be missing.

VIDEOS & PICTURES

I have many dreams but rarely remember a whole one. Most of the time, I'm left with pictures, like snapshots. Even one picture, like Instagram. Essentially I get a "highlights" reel. Maybe it is so with you. These are *"relational dreams"* in which God is letting us know He's thinking about us. There's no lesson, message, or correction. Yet we know there's a dream, so we know He's thinking of us.

On the other side of the spectrum, I have vivid dreams where I can recollect almost everything. These are longer — with action, a theme, and people — like a video clip. God gives these *"directional dreams"* when we're struggling. The degree of clarity is directly proportionate to the level of importance. Clear dreams give clear guidance, but only if I'm on a clear mission.

GOD'S DREAMS & HIS PURPOSES

God sends directional dreams at important junctures. I've already shared a few and God's purposes:

1. God gave me a series of dreams about the economic earthquake. His purpose was to prepare A-1 A-Lectrician and our people for the subprime failure.
2. God gave me a vision of an empty van to confirm my departure from Surfing the Nations.
3. God gave a dream to show me to relinquish all control to Jason. God's purpose was to have Jason depend on Christ alone as he runs A-1.
4. God gave Daven a dream about bread to show Daven He had designed and designated their home.
5. Missy's dream of a truck crash: God wanted Missy to know she was suffocating her daughter.
6. God gave Pastor Peter Brostek a dream about his future love, his bride "Ritzi."
7. God gave Diana a dream about Jesus to keep her from petty theft, and possibly much worse.

DOES GOD CONTROL HOW MUCH WE REMEMBER?

The Bible says that God is in control. That means He controls how much we remember in our dreams. In a "relational dream," God just wants us to know He's there with us. We don't remember much and that's okay because the dream is not the point, His presence is.

On the other hand, we can also tend to easily forget "directional dreams." Unless we write them down or act upon them. This is all part of God's plan to let us know He is there. He leaves it to us to seek

His wisdom in further prayer or through circumstances. The dream is not the only way He guides us, but it does provide a starting point. In my life, there may have been only about a dozen dreams that were pivotal. Yet they were critical to who I am today. Many were simply to encourage me and some "kicked me in the pants." God speaks over 90% without dreams. One might argue that God could work completely without dreams, but I like connecting with Him in Dreamland. It's neat!

The one thread uniting all of the people in the Bible is this: **They were all on God's journey**, whether they knew it or not. That journey provides context for God's dreams. It's the "Dream Decoder"!

CONTEXT, CONTEXT, CONTEXT!!!

There is a principle in real estate that successful investors follow: Location, Location, Location. Similarly, in successful dream interpretation, it is context, context, context. First the **global context** of the Bible. Then the more **refined context** of a specific book in the Bible. Then the **further refined context** of the chapter and *pericope*, or group of verses, that help present a unified thought or truth. Plus we have to integrate all of that with the context of what is happening in our lives. The Bible is not simple, but it is simpler than most other means of God's communication. The Bible is black and white. And to help break it down, there are many well-written commentaries and concordances. Yet it comes down to application. An important part of Bible study is in applying its lessons to our lives.

Mark Twain once said, "It ain't those parts of the Bible that I can't understand that bother me, it is the parts that I do understand."

If we simply live all that we understand of the Bible, we'll successfully fulfill His will. However, the Bible does not tell us who to marry, how many kids to have, how to roll toilet paper, how to squeeze toothpaste, where we should work, and whether I should leave my previous job that I loved to become a pastor in a Korean church next to Hawaii's largest public housing. I didn't see that!

The point is that the Bible is a starting point for a newly transformed life, but that's just what it is: only the beginning. **Living life with God daily is the rest and the best part.** Jesus calls us by name and we *"follow him because [we] know his voice"* (Jn. 10:3-4).

As Christians we believe what the Bible says about Jesus: *"In him was life"* (Jn. 1:4). We're to be satisfied in living with Him and hearing His voice. The rest is gravy. And yet I struggle with the simplicity of that. I battle with what it should look like and control sneaks in. I still want it my way.

God knows our struggles and doesn't hold it against us. With Jesus, we're not living under law but under grace (Gal. 3:24-25). So although we try to be perfect, God is more pleased that we're depending on Him for guidance, and He gives us that desire of our hearts.

One of my difficulties is that although God is always broadcasting; my tuner isn't always tuned in the right station. For instance, God wants to deal with my pride so He sends a message via discipline, my wife, or in my Bible reading. However, my focus elsewhere prevents me from receiving it. So I miss it.

We're not always ready to receive correction from God. Sometimes negative circumstances come as God works against me to humble me. Even greater, God knows He can reach me best when my defenses are down in my sleep. So dreams can be effective, but only as I'm receptive to His dreams.

CONTEXT OF MISSION, FAMILY, BUSINESS OR MINISTRY

When something goes wrong and blows up, I've learned that it's time to sit up and listen to God. Stop and ask, "What are You saying, Lord? What are You doing? What do You want me to do or do differently?

Is it my mission? Family? Ministry? Me?" Then, since I know He will guide my steps, I take a step. I observe if things get better. If it does, I take another step in the same direction. If not, ask God what are my options? Then I take another step. Life is fluid; flow with the situation. Just don't stay stuck.

Oftentimes, God confirms in my dreams what I already know: I need character change. So I think to myself: *Self, get going!* Or I pray, "Lord, help me do this." I also recognize that if God has something major to communicate in my dreams, He'll give me multiple dreams over a period of time. Or the dreams will interlock with life events like with Darrick and Missy's next step. Or He might choose to give multiple situations in the same dream with the same application. Grace abounds.

The key to understanding is to connect the dream to its proper context. Journaling dreams can help you spot patterns you may otherwise miss. It sounds like work, but God is worth it. God is a loving God and works with you in your gifts. The most important thing is to recognize and hear His voice.

Tom Bauer would say, "Whatever way you hear Him, just hear Him!"

LOOK FOR GOD'S CONNECTION

God always makes a solid connection when He sends dreams to impact your life, character, mission, or destiny. Our challenge is to find the connection. Look for what is important to you as His "connecting" point — history, culture, or values. Anything that connects may have meaning. Explore it, it'll be worth it.

One easy connection to make is a similarity to Biblical dreams (Ch. 2). Another easy connection is when you ask God to show you something specific, called "laying a fleece." Many dreams in this book made connections to God's direction. Once you get the connection, it's simply a matter of obedience.

In dreams, God uses connections that we are aware of, are meaningful to us, and are relevant to our current walk. *"Be still and know that He is God,"* (Ps. 46:10), in other words, **PAY ATTENTION!**

FLEECE: KNOWING FOR SURE

*"Abram said, 'O Sovereign Lord, **how can I know** that I will gain possession of it?'"* (Genesis 15:8)

*"The Lord answered, 'I will be with you, and you will strike down all the Midianites together.' Gideon replied, 'If now I have found favor in your eyes, **give me a sign that it is really you talking to me.**'"* (Judges 6:16-17)

As I write this, I think about all my Mom and Dad did for me: They allowed me to do whatever my heart desired and supported me all the way. They never pushed me into electrical engineering. They left that to God. (Though they didn't know Him then, God's Hand still guided them.)

What sticks out in my mind was the way Dad prepared me to join him in the business. Actually, he never even mentioned anything or tried any bribes. Yet I remember the call I made while I was working for Hughes Aircraft: "Dad, I'm coming home to work for the business." All he said was, "Okay."

There was no contract or negotiation about salary, car, or job responsibilities. I just came home and started working. I knew my Dad would pay me fairly. And he knew I'd be "all in." No need for discussion on either end. Now I think, *How did I know?* Well, I knew Dad — how he worked, what he thought, and what he expected. And, most importantly, I knew he believed in me. That was all I needed.

It must have been like that for Abraham and Gideon: Knowing was everything. Abraham believed what God said, that he would have offspring as many as the stars. Interestingly, he didn't find this odd at his old age, he only asked God how he could know that he would possess the land. So God answered with a vision familiar to Abraham: a sacrificial covenant. Gideon also needed to know it was really the Lord talking to him. Once he did, he was "all in."

We all come to a point where **knowing for sure** is the next level in God's mission. If we fall short or fail to go "all in," we take longer. That's bad in critical situations. Like jumping across a six-foot ravine but only half-heartedly; so you fall six-inches short. *Disaster!* On the other hand, you jump "all in"—leg muscles pumping, arms flailing, and yelling at the top of your lungs—and you make it! **Knowing makes all the difference.** Both Abraham and Gideon knew that if it was God who said so, it was done. The rest of their journey was not without trials and difficulties, but because they knew God, they continued to watch for His Hand. They had to walk the oft-lonely journey of faith, trusting God.

Asking God for a "fleece" to confirm His assignment, journey, or mission is Biblical. It was not weakness in Gideon nor is it weakness for a Christian who is on His mission and wants God to confirm the next major step. However, it is spiritual weakness to ask God to confirm the mission too often. That's double-minded. Once God sends an answer, He does not want us to keep asking for another and another and another confirmation. We're to walk out the journey with faith, confidence and courage.

For clarification, a **mission** is the global "big picture" for your life. It may last three years or five, maybe even 10. The **journey** is the current walk God has you on and may last one or two years. It's part of your long-term mission. An **assignment** is a short-term job and may last a few months.

"ENVISIONING WITH GOD"

One of my spiritual superheroes is **Pastor Francis Oda**, chair of Group 70 International; an architecture, engineering and design firm. Francis knows and trusts God. He has a process he calls, "Envisioning with God." Whenever he's on a mission, journey or assignment, he activates his intercessory prayer group. He then spends time **envisioning with God** in daily prayer, until he receives a vision. Sometimes God gives him an idea on a design way ahead of time. Sometimes God shows up one day or one week ahead; sometimes He shows up as he arrives at his meeting. Of course, God takes into account the time Francis needs to sketch the design or to finalize details. God knows all.

The key for Francis is that he knows God has chosen him to be an architect and a pastor. He also knows that God knows the designs and concepts He will download to Francis, in perfect time. Even if time runs out, Francis knows God will give the necessary time extension.

Francis' part is to depend on God completely. He must trust that God will guide him in his business (marketplace ministry) and in his church. Francis is "all in." Granted, not all of us are called to do what Abraham, Gideon or Francis were called to do, but we can do what God has called us to do.

LAY A FLEECE IN THE DIRECTION OF GOD'S PULL

There are two simple methods to laying a fleece: The first deals with a major decision or course correction. Try not to ask God a vague question, like, "Lord what do You want me to do?" Personally, I'm hard of hearing and need an advantage. It's much easier to ask God for something specific that relates to the journey I'm on. Such was the case of my Surfing the Nations fleece:

1. First, if I was released from a study, I asked God for a dream about an empty plate. I got one.
2. Second, I asked God for a dream involving a broken surfboard. He answered in a way I didn't expect: A surfing van without any surfboards. If I had not been specific, I might not have understood, but I did. Also, the timing of the dream happened on the same night that I asked for the fleece. God is good!

Keep your fleece simple and God will be able to speak simply in your dreams.

A second model for laying out a fleece is "**The Stop Dream.**" Start with a prayer, "God, I'm headed in a direction that I believe You're leading me towards. But if I'm on a wrong track that You do *not* desire, give me a dream and show me that You want me to stop." I lay out a specific scenario and if **I don't get that dream**, I know God answered in the affirmative and is blessing the journey; so I continue.

Jason used this in a huge project and since he didn't get the "STOP" dream he continued. He laid another fleece the next day and it also confirmed that same direction. In essence, we trust God and believe He will direct us to "STOP" if we stray off course. **If He doesn't speak, He SPOKE!**

JUST DREAM IT!

*"And they will tell the inhabitants of this land about it. They have already heard that you, O Lord, are with these people and that you, O Lord, have been seen **face to face**, that your cloud stays over them, and that you go before them in a pillar of cloud by day and a pillar of fire by night." (Numbers 14:14)*

God communicates in many ways but dreams are wonderfully personal. They tell us He is with us and that He hears our prayers; He even enjoys just "talking story"! It's similar to the Israelite experience — when God appeared to them *"face to face."* In my dreams, I feel like God is speaking to me *"face to face."* God can do miraculous things in our lives and in our world. This book has been about hearing God's voice. The better we hear, the more confident we are in our work and the stronger we are in our relationship with Him. It also helps us become more like Jesus.

We all walk with God through hearing from Him in our ears, in His Word, through visions and even dreams. The impact to our family, ministry, community and society is God's. The journey is ours.

May you be God's dream come true!

---

[1] Kolodiejchuk, Brian (2007) *Mother Teresa: Come Be My Light.* Crown Publishing Group.

[2] Lewis, C.S. (2015) *Mere Christianity.* Harper San Francisco.

[3] Metaxas, Eric. (2010) *Bonhoeffer: Pastor, Martyr, Prophet, Spy.* Nashville, TN, Thomas Nelson.

OTHER BOOKS BY JIMMY YAMADA, JR.

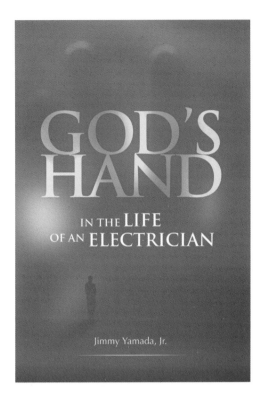

GOD'S HAND IN THE LIFE OF AN ELECTRICIAN (2008)

A great gift is to see God's hand on your life. In this life memoir, Jimmy Yamada, Jr. – a prominent Hawai'i businessman and ministry leader – looks back at the jagged shards of his past to see a clear pattern of God's design. And like sun streaming through a stained-glass cathedral, God truly makes all things good in His time. If God can do this for Jimmy Yamada, Jr., He can surely do it for you!

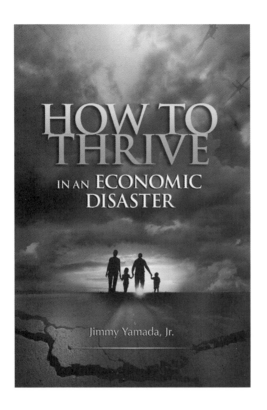

HOW TO THRIVE IN AN ECONOMIC DISASTER (2015)

Discover...
- Ways to prepare for a financial disaster
- Principles to help maneuver through your own calamities
- How God uses pain and suffering to develop strength and character
- Inspiring examples to apply lessons to your daily life

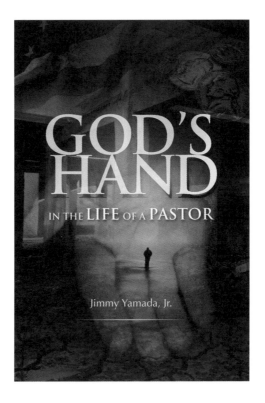

GOD'S HAND IN THE LIFE OF A PASTOR (2015)

This startling life story told in stark honesty is not one of fame and fortune. It's the nitty gritty reality of caring for the poorest of the poor in America. It's the dirt under God's fingernails as He points at you and asks: If not you, then **who**? If not now, then **when**?

WHITE
MOUNTAIN
CASTLE
PUBLISHING, LLC

www.whitemountaincastle.com